....k is to be returned on or before
.. date stamped below.

reserve

upheard

Preface books

A series of scholarly and critical studies of major writers intended for those needing modern and authoritative guidance through the characteristic difficulties of their work to reach an intelligent understanding and enjoyment of it.

General Editor: MAURICE HUSSEY

Available now:

A Preface to Wordsworth   BY JOHN PURKIS
A Preface to Donne   BY JAMES WINNY

Other titles in preparation

To the Noblest knight
Sr Edward Herbert.

Sr

I make account that thys Booke hath inough per=
formd wch yt undertooke, both by Argument and
Example. Jtt shall therfore the lesse neede to bee
ytt selfe another Example of ye Doctrine. Jtt shall
not therfore kyll ytt selfe. that ys, not bury it selfe.
for if ytt should do so, those reasons by wch that
Act should bee defended or excusd, were also lost
wt ytt. Since ytt ys content to liue, ytt cannot
chuse a wholsomer ayre then yor Library, where
Autors of all complexions are preserud. Jf any
of them grudge thys Booke a roome, and sus=
pect ytt of new or dangerous doctrine, yon, who
know us all, can best Moderate. To those Reasons
wch J know yor Loue to mee wyll make in my fauer,
and dischardge, yon may add thys, That though
thys Doctrine hath not beene tought nor defen=
ded by writers, yet they, most of any sorte of men
in the world, haue practisd ytt . —

                           yor uery true and earnest
                           frinde and seruant
                           and Louer

                                 J: Donne

Sample of Donne's writing, from a letter.

A Preface to Donne

James Winny

Longman

LONGMAN GROUP LIMITED
London

Associated companies, branches and representatives throughout the world

© Longman Group Ltd 1970

First published 1970

ISBN 0 582 31502 6 Cased
      0 582 31504 2 Paper

For Maurice

Photoset and printed in Malta by
St Paul's Press Ltd

Contents

Acknowledgements

For permission to reproduce photographs, we are grateful to the following: British Museum, pages 43, 63 and 71; Bodleian Library, pages 41 and 65; Country Life, page 107; Viscount De L'Isle, V.C., K.G., page 105; A. F. Kersting, Esq, pages 23 and 91; Most Hon. The Marquess of Lothian, for the cover picture; Mansell Collection, page 38; National Portrait Gallery, page 30; Science Museum, page 86; to publisher of Gosse: *Life and Letters of John Donne*, Heinemann, 1899, on page 13.

JAMES WINNY, Senior Lecturer in English at the University of Leicester, has edited several works by Chaucer and Renaissance writers. His most recent books have been devoted to the History Plays and Sonnets of Shakespeare.

List of Illustrations

Foreword

Mr Winny's book is intended for those, either at 'A' Level or above, who are fresh to the poetry of Donne and realize that critical guidance is essential before this intricate verbal art can communicate to us today—and this in spite of the fact that Donne has been claimed as modern for the last fifty years.

A number of intellectual, scientific, religious and artistic patterns is traced in the first four chapters. These may suggest to the reader that Donne is more medieval than modern, though the voice that emerges from the study and is present in the poems analysed in the fifth section is universal and compelling. We do not assume that the poetry is in any meaningful way *about* maps, mandrakes or compasses: nor are D. H. Lawrence's novels about the psychology of Freud. Donne and Lawrence, together with Shakespeare and Hardy, are pre-eminent in their definitions of the stages of love because of the sensitivity they show to the intellectual currents of their age as well as the power they possess of realizing emotional states.

Especially important in the present study, I believe, is the attempt to revise the common estimate of the poetry of the early seventeenth century, for years said to be the work of a 'school of Donne'. In Mr Winny's words: 'There could be no school of Donne, for his style was a uniquely personal instrument which could not serve the needs of other poets. What they took from him was at best a dilution of his racked and involved manner and more usually a domesticated form of the conceit which missed the inner logic of Donne's bizarre parallels and offered instead mere quaintness.' His philosophical ideas were largely familiar to educated people in 1590, but the attitudes taken up towards such inherited concepts are inimitably Donne's own. In order to equip the reader, who already has the sensibility, with the necessary information and then to blend both in his imaginative re-creation of the poetry has been the guiding principle in the preparation of this book.

General Editor: MAURICE HUSSEY

1 John Donne

Donne is not usually seen as a typical Elizabethan. Many of his readers, indeed, seem unready to associate him with the period of Elizabeth, and prefer to regard him primarily as a seventeenth-century poet, ignoring Ben Jonson's opinion that Donne wrote 'all his best pieces' before he was twenty-five, and thus before the end of the sixteenth century. It is not difficult to understand why the facts should be resisted. Donne's metaphysical style, with its bare scientific allusions and its insistently dialectical manner, seems almost completely at odds with the richly evocative language and the delight in natural creation that we find in Spenser, Marlowe and Shakespeare. Where their poetry expands imaginatively to take in great tracts of experience, Donne works tortuously towards a single, barely accessible point: his solution of a baffling intellectual problem.

If we associate the term 'Elizabethan' with discovery and colourful adventure, with richly textured speech and a sense of man's magnificence, it may be easy to feel that Donne falls short of the aureate quality that characterizes the literature of his age. His restless intellectual probing and questioning, we may feel, belong rather to the seventeenth century: not Shakespeare but Bacon is his contemporary in spirit. It is a commonplace of literary appreciation—not necessarily one to be approved—that the scientific interests revealed in Donne's poetry show him to be a forerunner of the new age of enquiry to which Bacon was herald. But it may be too readily assumed that references to spheres, maps and compasses demonstrate Donne's concern with the new science whose outlines Bacon seems to have perceived, or indeed that they indicate a scientific interest of any kind. The poets of the 1930s who mentioned gasworks and pylons were drawing attention to objects with a certain symbolic potency, not commenting on the progress of modern technology.

Shakespeare probably represents his age more completely than any other Elizabethan, but no one man can reflect every aspect of his times. Another writer may be strikingly unlike Shakespeare in style and outlook without ceasing to be typically Elizabethan. Such is Donne's case. The respects in which his thought and expression characterize the age will be discussed in later chapters of this book. For the moment, where we are concerned mainly with the biographical facts of his life, we shall find Donne typically Elizabethan in the uncertainty which dogged him throughout his career, in private belief as in material circumstances. He was born a Catholic at a time when increasing pressures were being applied to those of his faith, whose resistance endangered the newly established Anglican Church and its head, the Queen. No professing Catholic was allowed to take a degree at the two universities, nor could he hope for the kind of diplomatic or professional career to which an intelligent young man of good family was naturally inclined.

Donne's private difficulties as a Catholic epitomize the state of turbulence which England was going through during his early years. Since the reformation carried out by Henry VIII, the English Church had been twice set on contradictory courses, first under Mary who annulled all the religious changes introduced by the two previous monarchs, and then by Elizabeth who swept away Marian catholicism. When Donne was a young man there was no assurance that the Anglican Church would prove strong enough to withstand the attacks of its two enemies, Catholic and Puritan. Not only was the Anglican future in doubt: for many devout subjects of Elizabeth there were serious issues of conscience and political loyalty, and an anxious perplexity over the conflicting claims of several churches, all claiming sole authority:

> But unmoved thou
> Of force must one, and forc'd but one allow;
> And the right: ask thy father which is she,
> Let him ask his: though truth and falsehood be
> Near twins, yet truth a little elder is.

Donne's *Satire III*, in which these lines occur, proves the concern which he shared with the great body of Elizabethans who could not easily assure themselves that the form of religion authorized by the Queen was spiritually superior to the others, or that catholicism and true allegiance were incompatible. We see no evidence of this struggle in Shakespeare, even though his father may have been a recusant; and in this important respect Shakespeare proves a misleading guide to the human outlook of his times. The golden atmosphere of his early comedies may truly represent the optimism and self-confidence which the nation felt in its growing commercial strength and maritime daring, but Shakespeare gives no hint of the troubled spirit of the English Catholics, vainly trying to reconcile religious faith with their duty as loyal subjects of the Queen. For this aspect of Elizabethan life Donne acts as spokesman.

Donne's private career falls into two parts, separated by his decision at the age of forty-one to accept holy orders within the Anglican Church. The contrast between secular and religious in Donne is startling, as we might imagine by comparing one of the more scandalous of his love poems with one of the *Holy Sonnets*, or one of the many sermons which he preached as dean of St Paul's. As a student of Lincoln's Inn during the 1590s Donne was described as 'a great visitor of ladies, a great frequenter of plays', and although the writer conceded that he was 'not dissolute', the impudent and rebellious spirit of the poetry he wrote at this time suggests that this glimpse of his character as a young man does not misrepresent him. His first biographer, Isaak Walton, preferred to skirt this doubtful area of his subject and to concentrate attention upon the eagerness for study which

Donne was later to attribute to himself in these early years: 'an hydroptic immoderate desire of human learning and languages'; but Walton admits that after studying from four in the morning until ten, Donne then 'took great liberty'.

There is no need to censure Donne for taking the kind of wild pleasures that often form a complement to intense intellectual activity. In his case there might have been special reasons for seeking an outlet for the impetuous energies which his poetry reveals; for according to Walton, at this period Donne had not decided whether to continue a Catholic or not. The frustration and uncertainty of his position, which beside its effects on his future had the power to disturb his emotional being whichever decision he took, was a direct encouragement to Donne to lose himself temporarily in amusement and distraction. He seems not to have done things by halves. As the student was urged by an 'immoderate desire' for learning, so the playgoer was a 'great frequenter' of theatres and a great visitor of ladies.

The charged emotional nature was to remain when Donne became a churchman, but its energies were now turned upon a very different purpose. The element of rebellious protest conspicuous in his secular poetry, which overturns conventional attitudes and modes of expression and asserts a defiant individualism, is replaced by a conservative and authoritarian outlook as Donne upholds the rights of the established Church and its head, James I. If there are reasons for associating the Donne of the *Songs and Sonets* with the intellectual movements of a new age, there are equally strong arguments for seeing the dean of St Paul's as a figure of an age about to be eclipsed: a man whose anguished awareness of mortality and corruption seems to belong less to the period of Bacon than to the medieval past. In this paradoxical mixture Donne again characterizes his times.

Early career

If the second of these two figures dominates our impression of Donne, that is because we know so much less of the younger man. His family background at least is clear. He was born in 1572, the first son of a well-to-do London ironmonger who two years later was made head of his company. His father did not enjoy his prosperity very long, for he died soon after making his will in January 1576. Donne's mother, Elizabeth Heywood, was the daughter of a minor Elizabethan writer; and both parents were Catholics. Donne was to remark in *Pseudo-Martyr*, which argues against the readiness of English recusants to suffer for their faith, that no family had 'endured and suffered more in their persons and fortunes for obeying the teachers of Roman doctrine' than his own.

The Heywoods were particularly unfortunate. Donne's grandfather was obliged to flee the country, followed by Donne's uncle Elizaeus

Heywood, who after being mobbed at Antwerp died at Louvain in 1578. Another uncle, Jasper Heywood, who has some literary importance as a translator of Seneca, narrowly escaped being executed with five other Jesuit priests in 1584. He remained in prison until the summer of the year following, and was allowed to be visited by his sister, Donne's mother. Subsequently he was banished on pain of death if he returned to England, and died abroad before the end of the century. Before his uncle's death Donne had lost his younger brother Henry, who died of gaol fever in August 1593 after being imprisoned for harbouring a Catholic priest, William Harrington. Such family associations cannot have made it easy for Donne to abjure the faith for which his brother had died; though the fate of these relations showed the futility of his entertaining hopes of a distinguished career while he remained a Catholic.

Of Donne's early schooling nothing is known besides Walton's statement that 'a private tutor had the care of him' until he was ten. His widowed mother had been left rich enough to educate her son privately, and probably wished him to receive his first tuition from a teacher of her own faith. In the autumn of 1584, when Donne was about twelve, he and his brother Henry matriculated from Hart Hall, a university hostel at Oxford. Even by the standards of the time, this was making an early start with a university education, but there was good reason for haste. At the age of sixteen university students were required to take the Oath of Supremacy, which affirmed Elizabeth to be head of the Church in England. This conflicted directly with the Catholic position by repudiating the Pope's claim to the same authority, which no devout Catholic could do. To avoid exposing their sons to this public test of allegiance, many Catholic parents started them at university early enough for their education to be completed before the oath could be applied. This must have been the case with Donne and his brother, who were barred from taking a university degree by the same statutory declaration. Consequently Donne left Oxford, probably in 1588, without a degree, and remained without academic title until 1610, when the honorary degree of M.A. was conferred on him by his old university.

The next certain fact about Donne's career is his admission as a law student at Thavies Inn, London, in 1591, when he was nearly twenty. A period of three or four years between these two stages of education has not been accounted for. It has been suggested, by Grierson and Leishman among others, that Donne's residence of 'some years' in Spain and Italy, to which Walton refers imprecisely, occupied the period between Donne's studies at Oxford and London. Such an experience would have been valuable for any young man, and especially stimulating for a young poet; though we should not assume that Donne needed the stimulus of foreign travel and an exciting new literature to produce the poetry which he was almost certainly writing during the years 1591–96, as a student first at Thavies Inn and then at Lincoln's Inn.

ANNO DNI. 1591.
ÆTATIS SVÆ 18.

This was for youth, Strength, Mirth, and wit that Time
Most count their golden Age; but t'was not thine.
Thine was thy later yeares, so much refind
From youths Drosse, Mirth, & wit; as thy pure mind
Thought (like the Angels) nothing but the Praise
Of thy Creator, in those last, best Dayes.
    Witnes this Booke, (thy Embleme) which begins
    With Love; but endes, with Sighes, & Teares for sins.

Will: Marshall sculpsit.   IZ: WA:

Engraving of Donne as a young man.

If external stimulus was needed, Donne could have found enough excitement in the London of the 1590s, where an astonishing flowering of literary genius was taking place, and where every year Shakespeare gave more abundant proof of his greatness. The 'great visitor of plays' is unlikely to have missed any of those productions, first at the Theatre and later at the Globe, which made Shakespeare's name familiar to his first audiences. Some evident borrowings from Shakespeare's narrative poems, mentioned in another chapter of this book, suggest Donne's interest in the work of his great contemporary. London was a rapidly growing city, but a small one by our standards, and we can suppose that Donne soon made contact with the body of poets and dramatists whose creative vitality he shared. Jonson's opinion, already quoted, that Donne wrote all his best pieces before he was twenty-five, may imply that the men were acquainted before the end of this productive period, which coincides roughly with the date of Donne's materially disastrous marriage.

Like other readers of Donne's early poems, Jonson could only have read them in manuscript; for Donne did not publish his work. Perhaps he could not find a publisher for the *Songs and Sonets*, whose style and manner were so strikingly at odds with the late Petrarchan fashion of the time; or he may have wished to restrict their circulation as Shakespeare had done with his sonnets, by passing them round among his friends. The sonnets were eventually published, probably without Shakespeare's consent; but either Donne's name had not the public appeal which would induce a stationer to offer a pirated edition of Donne's love poems for sale, or his private circle of readers was completely trustworthy. When Francis Davidson compiled a list of 'Manuscripts to gett' in 1606 or thereabouts, he mentioned the 'Satyres, Elegies, Epigrams &c. by John Don', but seemed not to have heard of the love-poems.*

Walton's account of how Donne divided his time between study and relaxation is to be taken seriously. The intellectual interests to which Donne himself refers in the phrase 'immoderate desire of human learning' remained a vital part of his nature throughout his life, and directly influenced his poetic style. In the first of his *Satires*, probably written before 1594, Donne gives a wry picture of himself

> in this standing wooden chest,
> Consorted with these few books,

and runs through the categories which his library brings together:

> Here are God's conduits, grave divines; and here
> Nature's secretary, the philosopher;
> And jolly statesmen, which teach how to tie
> The sinews of a city's mystic body;
> Here gathering chroniclers, and by them stand
> Giddy fantastic poets of each land.

*He might, of course, have regarded them as satires, which some of them are.

The list comprises divinity, natural philosophy or science, politics, history and finally poetry, whose authors Donne affects to slight while admitting the quality which makes them congenial to him. It is a surprising revelation from the man whom we might know simply as the unreservedly passionate speaker of *The Sun Rising* or the outrageously designing lover of *The Flea*; and in our surprise at the range of Donne's academic interests we might think that his poetry was little more than a form of recreation directed by his studies. In fact the reverse is probably true. Donne's poetry compresses and epitomizes his whole experience as a man whose intellectual curiosity is as great as his susceptibility to passionate feeling. We should not therefore regard these poems as the fruits of a busy student's moments of leisure, which reflect his absorbed reading in divinity, law, natural history and other subjects. Donne's passion for learning seems to have been as intense as we might suppose his pursuit of woman to have been, if we took the love poems at their face value. His allusions to bookish ideas are no more academic, in the pejorative sense of the term, than his straightforward references to sex: the same passionateness impels both. Seen in this way, the *Songs and Sonets* provide a reliable picture of their author during a feverishly active and strikingly creative period from the age of twenty until his marriage in 1601.

This is not to say that the love poems are true in a literal or biographical sense. They may be, but it is unwise to assume it: the poetic 'I' is often an invention. In the appeal *To Christ* which can plausibly be taken as Donne's last poem, he might be speaking of youthful indiscretions which still weigh on his conscience:

> Wilt thou forgive that sin by which I've won
> Others to sin, and made my sin their door?
> Wilt thou forgive that sin which I did shun
> A year or two, but wallowed in a score?

On the other hand we have Baker's specific assurance that Donne 'lived at the Inns of Court, not dissolute but very neat', and evidence within the poems themselves of Donne's wish to shock his readers by standing current literary convention on its head rather than by disclosing his adventures as a great visitor of women. Clearly it suited Donne's temperament to assault and ridicule attitudes which most Elizabethan poets respected: to scoff where they venerated, to reject the habitual idealizing of woman and to present a creature of flesh and blood, as inconstant and dishonest as the lover who speaks his poem. There is no reason to suppose that this satirical attitude was the result of any actual disillusionment which Donne may have suffered. The reader senses that poetic convention, not woman, is the real target of Donne's iconoclasm, and he is left facing the more difficult problem of what should have aroused Donne's feelings against the literary fashion generally accepted by Elizabethan poets.

We have Walton's word that at this time Donne was 'unresolved what religion to adhere to'. The death of his brother in 1593 may have brought Donne to a spiritual crisis. If he remained loyal to the faith which had already denied him a university degree, it was not unlikely that his life would be wasted as fruitlessly as his brother's had been, whether as a victim of Catholic persecution in England or as a fugitive living to no purpose in a Catholic country abroad. A young man of intelligence and promise does not easily forgo the hopes of distinction and fortune which his natural talents could win; but nor does the son of a family which had stood firm under prolonged persecution easily abandon the faith which others had upheld with their lives. The argument in *Pseudo-Martyr*, that recusants who persist in their defiance are in effect committing suicide, seems an insult to the memory of Henry Donne. It also enables us to judge how much determination Donne had to bring to the task of justifying the course he eventually decided to take. Here too there could be no half-measures.

During the years at Lincoln's Inn the torturing dilemma was still unresolved. When we see the young poet doing his best to smash one of the accepted canons of Elizabethan writing—awed respect for the mistress— we are watching an arrogantly assured innovator compel the love lyric to accept a totally new idiom, and listening while Donne gives expression to the sense of angry frustration and protest by savaging an established convention of poetry. In this sense the *Songs and Sonets* may be considered autobiographical. They do not tell us how Donne spent his nights. They suggest how he felt as he struggled with the most testing problem which he would ever meet, and which could only be solved by clamping off a vital part of himself.

This satirical impulse in Donne was encouraged by a growing movement of complaint and protest among writers of the decade. Disillusion was in the air, and by 1599 the volume of satirical writing became so great that the Privy Council, alarmed by the spread of libellous and defamatory pamphlets, forbade the publication of any further satires. Like most works of this kind, the five satires written by Donne before the end of the century are blunt and vigorously abusive; and most of their energy is directed against a society grown corrupt and vicious. So, after a visit to the court in *Satire IV*, Donne ruminates over the suitors whom he has seen there,

> and a trance
> Like his who dreamt he saw hell did advance
> Itself on me: such men as he saw there
> I saw at court, and worse, and more. Low fear
> Becomes the guilty, not the accuser: then
> Shall I, none's slave, of high-born or raised men
> Fear frowns? and, my mistress Truth, betray thee
> To the huffing braggart, puffed nobility?
> No, no: thou, which since yesterday hast been
> Almost about the whole world, hast thou seen,
> O sun, in all thy journey, vanity
> Such as swells the bladder of our court?

A settled rhythm is never allowed to establish itself in these lines, whose jerky movement strengthens the impression of the speaker's impatience and disgust. It is not only in his formal satires that Donne adopts this disturbed manner. Some of the most effective of the *Songs and Sonets* are maliciously satirical in purpose and expression, demonstrating at once Donne's personal power and the destructiveness which, as in *The Apparition*, springs from the frustration of his urge towards fulfilment. Even when, as in *The Sun Rising*, he has found complete sexual satisfaction, the satirical impulse cannot be silenced and must express itself in violent abuse of the sun, whom the lover derides as 'busy old fool' and 'saucy pedantic wretch'. In this way the language of satire runs through Donne's writing of this period, as though the angry perplexity of his private dilemma was continually demanding and finding a voice.

If we accept Jonson's judgment of this early work, we may think that the strain of this spiritual crisis contributed to the success of Donne's poetry during this tortured and decisive period of his life. Exasperation seems to have been converted into poetic energy, giving Donne's writing its thrusting impetus: a wilful force which the discipline of metre barely controls. His poems often reveal an explosive power of feeling held under pressure and determined to find an outlet, twisting and wrenching itself to reach the solution of a self-imposed problem. It may not be fanciful to suppose that the discordance of Donne's verse, and the tortuousness of his arguments, reflect his state of mind as a Catholic torn between desperate alternatives, either of which would permanently maim him.

As an Anglican apologist, Walton makes light of Donne's spiritual trouble and implies that Donne had only to apply himself to a comparison of the two faiths to recognize which was authentic: 'Indeed, truth had too much light about her to be hid from so sharp an enquirer, and he had too much ingenuity not to acknowledge he had found her.' Donne's own account of his struggle in *Pseudo-Martyr* conflicts with this suggestion of an easy victory for truth. Those who know him, he asserts, are aware 'that I used no inordinate haste nor precipitation in binding my conscience to any local religion'; and he goes on:

I had a longer work to do than many other men, for I was first to blot out certain impressions of the Roman religion, and to wrestle both against the examples and against the reasons by which some hold was taken, and some anticipations early laid, upon my conscience; both by persons who by nature had a power and superiority over my will, and others who by their learning and good life seemed to me justly to claim an interest for the guiding and rectifying of mine understanding in these matters.

Donne is writing diplomatically, but his allusions allow us to read a little between the lines. The persons 'who by nature had a power and superiority' over him can only be members of his family, notably his mother who outlived him by dying in 1632, still a staunch Catholic. The 'examples' given by his close relations need not be enumerated. The 'reasons' seem to have come partly from his parents and partly from teachers, perhaps those responsible for his early education. When Donne speaks of the 'learning and good life' which influenced him, he may be covertly admitting that Catholic priests played some part in this schooling. With all these forces working against the urge to break with his Catholic upbringing, Donne might well confess how difficult it was for him to 'blot out' the persuasions which had formed his outlook since childhood, and what anguished wrestling led to his eventual decision to leave the Catholic Church. When the break occurred we do not know. Donne's third satire, which deals with the problem of finding the true religion, is generally ascribed to the period 1593–4. It offers no ready answer. 'Seek true religion: O where?' the poet asks; and the best solution he can offer himself is to persist in serious enquiry:

> Be busy to seek her: believe me this,
> He's not of none, nor worst, that seeks the best.
> To adore or scorn an image, or protest,
> May all be bad: doubt wisely: in a strange way
> To stand enquiring right is not to stray;
> To sleep or run wrong is.

The answer is unlikely to have come suddenly, or to have left Donne spiritually at peace with himself. Towards the end of this poem he asks himself abruptly whether he is content to let his soul be tied

> To man's laws, by which she shall not be tried
> At the last day? O will it then boot thee
> To say a Philip or a Gregory,
> A Harry or a Martin* taught thee this?
> Is not this excuse for mere contraries
> Equally strong? cannot both sides say so?

The final uncertainty of any solution could be countered only by a readiness to believe without question, and *Satire III* makes it clear that Donne was unable to give this kind of total assent. To the end of his life he continued to search for the assurance that only faith can give; seeking proof of divine mercy and trying to argue himself into a conviction that his soul might be saved. After more than fifteen years' priestly service within the Anglican Church, Donne's uncertainty had not been silenced. His ambitions had found some belated satisfaction, though not in a form which the young man could have foreseen, but he had exchanged catholicism for a faith to whose truth only his intellect seems to have responded.

In 1596, perhaps no longer a practising Catholic, Donne left Lincoln's Inn and the London playhouses to take part in an expedi-

*Meaning the king of Spain, the Pope, Henry VIII and Luther.

18

Map showing England, Cadiz and the Azores.

ENGLAND

ITALY

SPAIN

Cadiz

THE AZORES

tion against Cadiz, commanded by Essex. The fleet, comprising over eighty ships and at least six thousand trained men, reached Cadiz on 20 June and took the city completely by surprise. The attacking forces overran the Spanish defences, and to prevent a treasure-fleet in the harbour from falling into English hands, the Spaniards were obliged to sink their ships and a cargo valued at twelve million ducats. Essex withdrew his forces two weeks later, having sacked and fired the city; and before leaving Spanish waters sacked two more enemy towns. After this resounding success, a second expedition was organized in July of the following year, under Essex. His orders were to attack and destroy the ships being assembled at Ferrol in northern Spain as a second armada against England, and then to intercept the Spanish treasure-fleet at the Azores. But Essex and his fellow-commanders Howard, Vere and Ralegh were not to repeat their success of the previous year. Their expedition encountered a great gale which drove them back to port, and when they were again able to put to sea the projected attack on Ferrol had been put off. The fleet sailed directly for the Azores, where in September it failed to make its planned interception of the Spanish treasure-ships, which made safe harbour in the islands. Essex returned to England with nothing accomplished.

Donne sailed with both expeditions, in what capacity is not known. A taste of military service formed part of the liberal education of a sixteenth-century gentleman, who was expected to have some proficiency in all the main fields of human endeavour. Ophelia, we remember, sees Hamlet as a combination of courtier, soldier, and scholar: a diversity of accomplishment which after his experiences in 1596 and 1597 Donne could have claimed too. But Donne is not likely to have sailed with Essex for the sake of military glory, or to widen his experience as a poet; though the great storm which dispersed the Islands expedition provided the matter of a poem mocking the plight of ships and men:

> Some coffined in their cabins lie, equally
> Grieved that they are not dead, and yet must die;
> And as sin-burdened souls from graves will creep
> At the last day, some forth their cabins peep,
> And tremblingly ask what news, and do hear so—
> Like jealous husbands—what they would not know.

A companion poem, *The Calm*, won praise from Jonson, who was generally unsympathetic towards Donne's work. A well-educated Elizabethan gentleman of twenty-five, as Donne now was, must have hoped to attract favourable attention from one of the many noble and influential men of affairs which the expeditions brought together, and to be entered upon the career in public life which, with his abandoning of the Catholic faith, was now open to him. Walton tells us that Donne waited upon Essex, which may mean that he sought his patronage; but any hopes of preferment which Essex may have encouraged came to an end in 1601, when Essex paid the penalty for his abortive uprising against the Queen.

By this date Donne had in fact established himself in a position of considerable promise. One of his companions on both the voyages was Thomas Egerton, whose father was Keeper of the Great Seal and Lord High Chancellor. From a letter written by Donne four years later it appears that his friend brought Donne to his father's notice, with the result that he was appointed secretary to Sir Thomas Egerton. 'Taking notice of his learning, languages and other abilities, and much affecting his person and behaviour', as Walton tells us, Sir Thomas 'took him to be his chief secretary, supposing and intending it to be an introduction to some weighty employment in the state, for which his lordship* did often protest he thought him very fit.'

Donne's star had now risen, and with this auspicious beginning to a secular career there seemed no reason why his abilities should not have carried him to the kind of position in state affairs which Egerton had in mind. An important further step was taken in October 1601 when Brackley, a constituency controlled by Egerton, returned Donne as one of its members of Parliament; but before the end of the same year Donne saw his hopes suddenly and irretrievably ruined by a single impulsive action of his own. Since 1596 Egerton had been acting as guardian to Ann More, whose father Sir George More was Lieutenant of the Tower of London. Ann, it appears, entered the Egerton household when her aunt married Donne's employer, and continued to live there after her aunt's death in 1600. In this changed state of affairs Ann probably found rather more personal liberty than hitherto, and was now of an age to attract male interest. She and Donne fell in love, and Ann accepted his proposal of marriage. As Donne was later to acknowledge in a letter to her outraged father, he knew that he could not expect Sir George to accept him as prospective son-in-law. He was not yet able to support a wife in the circumstances which Sir George would require for his daughter; and in addition it seems that Sir George had taken an instinctive dislike to him. Knowing that to reveal their plans would have been, in Donne's phrase, 'to impossibilitate the whole matter', the lovers were married secretly in December 1601; Ann being then seventeen and her husband twenty-nine.

Marriage

This romantic but reckless step could not be immediately admitted. By marrying Ann without her father's consent Donne had committed offences against both common law and canon law, and he was naturally anxious not to disclose his secret until Sir George had been carefully prepared to learn of his daughter's marriage. The truth was eventually revealed to him by his friend the Earl of Northumberland, who had agreed to act as Donne's emissary, and who carried a letter

---

*Walton anticipates: Egerton was subsequently created Lord Ellesmere.

from Donne begging his father-in-law to deal with the situation 'as the persuasions of nature, reason, wisdom and Christianity' should direct him. The plea was disregarded. The news, Walton relates, was so 'immeasurably unwelcome' to Sir George that he was transported with rage; and with complete inconsideration both for Donne and for his daughter he set about revenging himself by ruining his son-in-law's hopeful prospects. His first step was to persuade Sir Thomas Egerton, by means which Walton does not properly explain, to dismiss Donne from his service. He lost such a secretary, Egerton is reported to have said, 'as was fitter to serve a king than a subject': a compliment which if sincere suggests what pressure Donne's enraged father-in-law was able to bring to bear upon his employer. Donne seems to have realized that his dismissal meant the collapse of his fortunes, for the letter which he wrote to his wife telling her this bad news concluded with an epigram which summed up their wretched position: 'John Donne, Ann Donne, undone.'

But worse was to come. Still smarting with anger, Sir George continued his persecution by having Donne committed to prison, together with the two friends who had taken part in the marriage ceremony. Donne at once wrote to his father-in-law expressing his penitence and submission, and remarking that although Sir George might not intend 'utter destruction, yet the way through which I fall towards it is so headlong that, being thus pushed, I shall soon be at the bottom'. This appeal had no effect, but after Donne had begged for help from Sir Thomas Egerton he was allowed to leave prison, though not to enjoy complete liberty. As his spirits revived, he began to hope that he might be reconciled with his father-in-law and readmitted to Egerton's service. The first of these hopes was answered, for Sir George was slowly induced to take a more favourable view of the man who had captured his daughter. One of Donne's spokesmen was his friend Christopher Brooke, a young lawyer who after giving away the bride at Donne's wedding had been imprisoned in the Marshalsea at her father's suit. After two weeks' imprisonment he wrote to Sir George asking to be released on the security of £1100, and including a plea for Donne: 'Were it not now best that everyone whom he anyway concerns should become his favourer or his friend who wants, my good lord, but fortune's hands and tongue to rear him up and set him out?' The commendations of Donne by men whose judgment Sir George could not ignore, and the personal attraction which Walton describes as 'a strange kind of elegant irresistible art', eventually broke down his father-in-law's resistance, and Sir George then tried to mend the harm he had done by persuading Sir Thomas Egerton to reinstate his former secretary.

In this more vital matter Donne's hopes were to be disappointed. Possibly because he had been roughly treated by More in his determination to secure Donne's dismissal, Egerton was not disposed to do his bidding a second time; especially when this involved reversing his original decision. At all events, More was told that although Sir

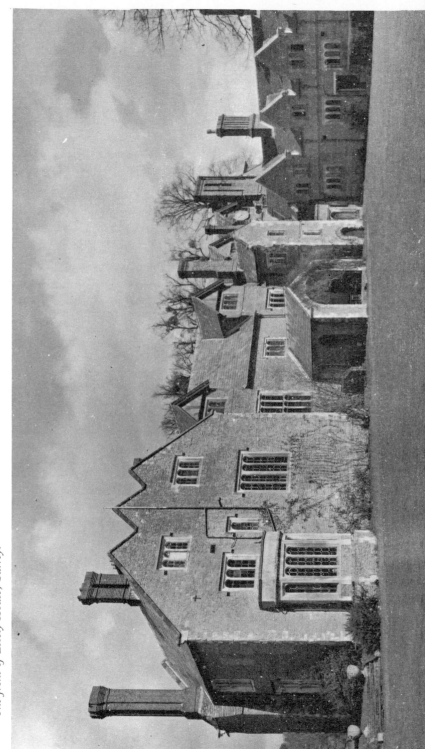

The front of Losely House, Surrey.

Thomas was 'unfeignedly sorry for what he had done, yet it was inconsistent with his place and credit to discharge and readmit servants at the request of passionate petitioners'. The explanation does not ring completely true, for such yielding to pressure does not become undignified only when it is repeated; but there was no consolation for Donne in that. After a long and costly law-suit he had managed to obtain possession of his wife, who had been held by her father while a special commission was considering whether her marriage was legally binding. The court gave its verdict, favourable to Donne, in April 1602, more than sixteen months after their clandestine marriage; but though the couple had the happiness of reunion and life together, their future held no certainty besides their love for one another. Donne had good reason to adopt the attitude of the speaker in many of his love poems, who insists that he and his mistress constitute in themselves the whole world.

It would be pleasant to believe that after this period of shared adversity Donne and his young wife enjoyed the kind of mutual dependence and understanding which he describes in the tenderest and most convincing of his love poems. Walton's story of Donne's vision of his wife 'with her hair hanging about her shoulders, and a dead child in her arms', when she gave birth to a stillborn child during his absence abroad, suggests a remarkable closeness of relationship. But the anecdote has another significance. Children came in rapid succession to the Donnes as to most Elizabethan families. 'I stand like a tree,' he wrote to a prospective godfather in 1615, 'which once a year bears though no fruit, yet this mast* of children.' The tone of his remark seems not entirely playful. The straitness of Donne's circumstances during much of his married life meant that every fresh increase in his family strained his resources a little further. Parents and children were repeatedly troubled by illness, and Ann Donne's strength was progressively worn down by childbearing and its attendant troubles. A letter written by Donne in 1614 gives a sombre picture of a household crushed by accumulated cares.

> There is not one person besides myself in my house well. I have already lost half a child, and with that mischance of hers [a miscarriage] my wife fallen into an indisposition which would afflict her much, but that the sickness of her children stupefies her; of one of which, in good faith, I have not much hope. This meets a fortune so ill-provided for physic and such relief, that if God should ease us with burials I know not well how to perform even that. I flatter myself in this, that I am dying too; nor can I truly die faster by any waste than by loss of children.

Protracted misfortune and worry test and sometimes break what was previously the strongest love. In the explanatory letter sent through his go-between to Sir George More, Donne had remarked

*Acorns, beechnuts etc.

24

and he and his wife 'both knew the obligations that lay upon us, and we adventured equally': though not, we may feel, with the expectation of such lasting distress as their adventure brought them. If Donne's secular ambitions had been a decisive factor in his rejection of the catholic faith, they are unlikely to have allowed him to marry Ann More in the knowledge that he was risking all that he had gained by this renunciation. He must have reckoned that Ann's father would reluctantly accept his *fait accompli*; and he could not have foreseen that Egerton would be coerced into dismissing him. It is not entirely cynical of J. B. Leishman to suggest that although Donne loved his wife, he could not conceal from himself that she had brought misfortune upon him, as he upon her. Donne certainly admitted his responsibility for Ann's depressed state of life. Writing to a friend in 1608, he explains that the letter has not been composed in 'my poor library' nor on the highway 'where I am contracted and inverted into myself'—his two usual places of contemplation—but from the fireside in his parlour,

> in the noise of three gamesome children, and by the side of her whom, because I have transplanted her into a wretched fortune, I must labour to disguise that from her by all such honest devices as giving her my company and discourse; therefore I steal from her all the time which I give to this letter.

This glimpse of Donne's domestic life after seven years of marriage hardly corresponds with the conception of lovers completely unified and 'interassured of the mind' which he gives in one of the most touching of his poems. With the evidence of Donne's concern to comfort his wife by distracting her attention from the realities of their situation, we may wonder whether his 'honest devices' did not include some of the poems apparently addressed to her: sincere rather in their wish to alleviate a distress of spirit than in their assertion of a relationship which adversity could not injure.

Burdened with more immediate cares, Ann Donne may not have recognized her husband's still greater need of the help which he tried to give her. The ruin of his ambitious hopes left a permanent mark upon him, and Donne seems to have convinced himself that his life had effectively come to an end in 1601. 'I have been no coward, nor unindustrious,' he wrote to Sir Henry Wotton in 1612, 'nor will I give it over yet'; but after this show of determination the letter continues: 'If at last I must confess that I died ten years ago . . . at a blow, then when my courses were diverted, yet it will please me a little to have had a long funeral, and to have kept myself so long above ground without putrefaction.' This grim quip might be taken as a flash of witty self-mockery, no more essentially serious than the lover's remark in *The Legacy*, who dies 'as often as from thee I go'; but the contradictory impulses of Donne's nature habitually lead him to present serious beliefs in a wrily comic form. He had made use of the conceit of being already dead in writing to Sir Henry Goodyer in 1608, again after referring to the ruin of his career:

And there I stumbled too, yet I would try again; for to this hour I am nothing, or so little that I am scarce subject and argument good enough for one of mine own letters. Yet I fear that doth not ever proceed from a good root, that I am so well content to be less—that is, dead.

'I would fain do something,' he admits in the same letter, 'but that I cannot tell what is no wonder. For to choose is to do; but to be no part of anybody is to be nothing.' Again it is hard not to reflect that the love-poems tell a different story: there Donne is part of a composite being which encloses a totality of existence, and becomes 'the grave of all that's nothing' only when, in *A Nocturnal upon St Lucy's Day*, death, puts an end to this vital relationship of selves.* If he was consistent in trying to reassure his wife, Donne may not have disclosed to her the morbid depression which found some outlet in his correspondence. His melancholy sense of being nothing, or a man already dead and enduring an extended funeral, helps to explain what moved him to write his *Biathanatos*, an elaborate treatise in defence of suicide, during these difficult years. So far as his letters allow us to look into his domestic life at this time, they do not show that love brought him any real consolation for the collapse of his hopes, or that Ann Donne was able to secure him against the blackness of spirit which settled upon him as the emptiness of his existence deepened.

The first two years of the Donnes' life together were spent at Purford, a few miles from Guildford in Surrey. Two children, Constance and John, had been born to them when in 1605 they settled at Mitcham, a small town 'noted for good air and choice company' some eight miles south of London Bridge, now swallowed up in Greater London. Donne appears to have divided his time between his home and growing family—'mine hospital at Mitcham', as he was to describe it when sickness struck them—and a lodging in the Strand which afforded him some contact with men whose influence and position might benefit him. Walton asserts that 'his acquaintance and friendship were sought for by most ambassadors of foreign nations', but the only employment which Donne is known to have obtained was that of assisting one of the King's chaplains, Thomas Morton, in the task of persuading the English recusants to give up their faith. Donne must have felt the irony of his position. While at Lincoln's Inn he had undertaken a searching enquiry into the controversy between Anglican and Catholic over points of doctrine; primarily, we may suppose, in order to convince himself intellectually that it would be right to free himself of the disability which catholicism placed upon him. The special knowledge which he had acquired by this study was now useful to the established Church, and instead of regaining a position leading to employment by the state, Donne found himself drawn back into the religious conflict from which he had emerged a decade earlier. There

*It is not at all certain that this poem relates to the death of Ann Donne. Lucy was the name of Donne's patroness the Countess of Bedford.

Part of Speed's map of Surrey, showing London, Losely, Mitcham, Purford and Twickenham.

was more than irony in the fact that Donne was now engaged as an agent of Catholic apostasy. Whether good or bad, his own decision to leave the Catholic community had come from within himself, as a choice dictated by his own reason. Those recusants whom Morton's tracts persuaded were acted upon by others; and if they sinned their guilt was shared by the assistant who helped Morton to compile his scholarly arguments. This is the more likely context of Donne's plea in his poem *To Christ*:

> Wilt thou forgive that sin by which I've won
> Others to sin, and made my sin their door?

The sin which became 'their door' was Donne's own renunciation of Catholic faith: an example which could be used to induce other recusants to give way. This reading of *To Christ* would imply that, despite his priesthood within the Anglican Church, Donne remained a Catholic at heart to the end of his life. This is not inconceivable; for while he seems to have convinced himself intellectually of the truth of Anglican doctrine, his intuitive acceptance of catholicism could not be altered. The anguish of Donne's religious verse, of which the present instance is typical, seems attributable to this conflict of faith within himself.

Donne may have disliked his work as Morton's assistant for a number of reasons, not least because it led in a direction opposite to his ambitions; and certainly because what it showed of his learning and abilities convinced Morton that Donne was needed within the church, where his talents would find full employment. When Morton was appointed dean of Gloucester in 1607 he suggested to Donne that he should take orders, offering as inducement to resign a profitable benefice in Donne's favour if he would agree. After three days' meditation, Walton relates, Donne declined; partly through fear that 'some irregularities' of his past life might be notorious enough to bring disgrace upon the Church if he were made priest, and partly because if he accepted, it might be from his eagerness to escape poverty rather than from a wish to serve God.

Donne may not have declared himself with complete frankness. According to Walton, Morton had opened his proposal by referring to Donne's expectation of state employment, and by admitting his fitness for such a post. It might seem strange that Donne did not himself allude to this long-sustained hope in his reply; for if it were still alive he cannot have wished to compromise this ambition by accepting an appointment in the Church. He may have concealed another motive for declining Morton's offer, hinted at in the comment which Walton attributes to him: 'Happy is that man whose conscience does not accuse him for that thing which he does.' Donne's resistance to the growing pressure put upon him to enter the Church, up to his capitulation in 1615, suggests that besides his unwillingness to forgo his major ambition he felt some serious moral aversion to taking orders. We are brought back again to the crucial decision which he made as a young man. If the issue had been between religious faith and secular ambition, he had made a choice which probably never ceased to trouble him, whether consciously or not. His anglicanism was not insincere, but it did not reach down to the deeper levels of his emotional being from which his catholicism had never been properly evicted. The sense of strain and unrest so habitual in his writing probably derives from this deep-seated conflict within himself. Evidently he could accommodate himself to the spiritual tension which the half-acknowledged sin of renouncing his early faith incurred; but his resistance to the step proposed by Morton in 1607, and by the King himself after the publication of *Pseudo-Martyr* in 1610, suggests that Donne could not contemplate any further and much graver compromise.

A year after his refusal of Morton's offer, Donne was relieved of his most pressing material anxiety. Sir George More was at last prevailed upon to make provision for his daughter, whose dowry he had hitherto refused to pay. He now bound himself to pay Donne eight hundred pounds at some future date as Ann's wedding-portion, and meanwhile to pay interest on this sum at the rate of twenty pounds a quarter. By Jacobean standards, eighty pounds a year was a very fair income; equivalent to at least a thousand pounds of modern money. Not only was the family now secure against the poverty which had dogged Donne since marriage, but Donne was able to resume a modest place in society. His friendship with the Countess of Bedford, who acted as godmother to Donne's second daughter in 1608, seems to date from this time. Donne's letters show him frequently visiting Twickenham Park, where 'the good Countess' lived, and several of his poems are addressed to her. They are not the most compelling of Donne's works for a modern reader, out of sympathy with the elaborately complimentary manner of Donne's age; but they contain some gracefully turned conceits whose delicacy may surprise us after the aggressive style of the *Songs and Sonets*. So, in one of these verse letters, he tells her:

> You, for whose body God made better clay,
> Or took soul's stuff such as shall late decay,
> Or such as needs small change at the last day:
> This, as an amber drop enwraps a bee,
> Covering discovers your quick soul, that we
> May in your through-shine front your heart's thoughts see.

Walton does not admit that London and courtly society held any attraction for Donne at this time, and asserts that Donne would gladly have immersed himself in his theological studies at Mitcham. This opinion is not supported by a letter written to Sir Henry Goodyer in 1609. 'You, living at court without ambition,' Donne tells his friend, 'live in the sun, not in the fire; and I, which live in the country without stupefying, am not in darkness but in shadow; which is not no light, but a pallid, waterish and diluted one.' By speaking in the same letter

29

of 'the barbarousness and insipid dullness' of the country, Donne shows how unwillingly he had suffered his enforced exile from the city and the society in which he had moved as a young man. Friendship with the Countess of Bedford offered Donne the *entrée* to a circle of noble and distinguished families through whom his ambitions might still be fulfilled, and with whom he might enjoy the cultured pleasures which Mitcham did not afford. His refusal of Morton's proposal might now have seemed fortunate, but Donne was not yet to realize that Morton's high opinion of his abilities had been passed on to the King, and that James was determined to secure his services for the Church.

Among the many new acquaintances which Donne formed as his social horizon widened was Sir Robert Drury, a man of great wealth and ambition who had hopes of marrying his daughter Elizabeth to Prince Henry, the King's eldest son. In 1610 Elizabeth Drury died aged fifteen, leaving her father overwhelmed with grief. Donne had never met the daughter, and at the time of her death he may not have been acquainted with Sir Robert; but lack or slightness of familiarity with the family did not prevent him from composing an elegy of several hundred lines eulogizing the dead girl in the most strained and hyperbolic terms. In Jonson's opinion this poem was 'profane and full of blasphemies'. He told Donne that 'if it had been written of the Virgin Mary it had been something'; to which Donne answered that he had 'described the idea of a woman, and not as she was'. It might have been more honest if Donne had admitted that the poem had been designed to make one of the richest men in England his patron, for it is difficult to see any other motive in his noisy, repeated insistence that all the world's ills and disorders spring from Elizabeth Drury's death:

> She to whom this world must itself refer
> As suburbs, or the microcosm of her,
> She, she is dead, she's dead: when thou know'st this,
> Thou know'st how lame a cripple this world is;
> And learn'st thus much by our anatomy,
> That this world's general sickness doth not lie
> In any humour, or one certain part;
> But as thou saw'st it rotten at the heart . . .
> For the world's subtlest immaterial parts
> Feel this consuming wound, and age's darts;
> For the world's beauty is decayed or gone.

The pessimism which Donne proclaims so tirelessly in *The First Anniversary* was probably not assumed. His letters over the preceding years admit a growing melancholy; a weariness of life which he claimed to have felt when he 'went with the tide and enjoyed fairer hopes than now'. Although he can have felt nothing for Elizabeth Drury, her death gave him an occasion for expressing the deep misgivings which he shared with many Jacobean writers who saw the old order of life being steadily undermined by new

Portrait of Donne in a ruff, by Isaak Oliver, 1617.

habits of thought and belief. The best-known passage of *The First Anniversary*, in which Donne touches on the disturbing activities of the new astronomers, reveals a force of personal anxiety which almost carries his hyperbolic elegy on the dead girl:

> And freely men confess that this world's spent,
> When in the planets and the firmament
> They seek so many new: they see that this
> Is crumbled out again to his atomies.
> 'Tis all in pieces, all coherence gone,
> All just supply, and all relation:
> Prince, subject, father, son, are things forgot;
> For every man alone thinks he hath got
> To be a phoenix, and that then can be
> None of that kind of which he is, but he.

The First Anniversary was published, with Donne's authority though apparently against his better judgment, in 1611: the first of his poems to be printed. By then its open appeal for Sir Robert's patronage had been successful, and Donne and his family were living rent-free in his new patron's house in Drury Lane, midway between the cities of Westminster and London proper. The 'elegant, irresistible art' exercised by Donne in his youth seems still to have been effective; for in 1611 Sir Robert proposed that Donne should accompany himself and his wife on a visit to France and the Low Countries which would take them away for several months. Ann Donne was expecting a child and was unwilling to be left, but Walton makes it appear that Sir Robert would not take no for an answer, and that eventually Donne's wife reluctantly gave her consent. Donne may have felt that Sir Robert's patronage was too valuable to be jeopardized by resisting his wishes, or his eagerness to travel may have overcome his husbandly feelings.

He was out of England from the end of 1611 until at least August of the following year, residing with the Druries at Amiens, Paris and Brussels. It was during his absence, in January 1612, that Ann Donne gave birth to a stillborn child and Donne saw the vision recorded by Walton, in which she twice passed through the room carrying her dead baby. According to his biographer, Donne immediately sent to England for news of his wife, and learnt twelve days later that she had been delivered on the same day as her visionary self had appeared to him. But Walton is mistaken, for a letter written by Donne early in April remarks that he had received 'no syllable, neither from herself nor by any other, how my wife hath passed her danger'. It seems that the story of Donne's vision must be apocryphal; and this lack of correspondence again leaves us wondering whether his relations with Ann were as close as some of his poems imply.*

*To be fair to Donne, we should take account of his comment in a letter of 1614, referring to himself and his wife: 'We had not one another at so cheap a rate as that we should ever be weary of one another.' But the remark is not entirely compatible with this long absence from her.

By September 1612 Donne was back in London, still without the position which had tantalized his hopes for so long, and apparently ready to abandon the ambition on which he had wasted himself. Now aged forty, Donne addressed an appeal to Robert Carr, a royal favourite whom James had recently created Viscount Rochester; telling him that he had resolved to make his profession divinity, and asking for his assistance. Presumably this was Donne's indirect way of bringing himself to the notice of James, who after reading *Pseudo-Martyr* had tried like Morton to persuade Donne to enter the Church. If so, he was disappointed, for nothing came of Donne's appeal besides Rochester's general patronage, admitted in a later letter when Donne speaks of having 'lived upon your bread' since their first meeting, a year before. Donne was now writing to ask the favourite to use his influence to have him appointed to the vacant post of ambassador at Venice, but this too fell through. In 1614 he was elected a Member of Parliament for Taunton, and sat during the nine weeks of its assembly in early summer. He seems to have had some other business afoot at this time, for writing to his brother-in-law at the end of July Donne complains that the arrival of a Danish embassy at court has interrupted his plans: 'Their coming have put my little court business out of the way, and dispossessed me of so near hopes as lacked little of possession. . . . I must confess my weakness in this behalf,' he adds; 'no man attends court fortunes with more impatience than I do.'

His waiting was nearly over. Later that year, probably as the result of renewed appeals to Rochester, now the Earl of Somerset, he was invited to Theobalds in Essex, where the King was residing, and promised the post of clerk to the Council which had just fallen vacant. Somerset spoke as though James could not deny his request, but he had not reckoned with the King's private purposes. 'I know Mr Donne is a learned man, has the abilities of a learned divine, and will prove a successful preacher,' he told Somerset, 'and my desire is to prefer him that way; and in that way I will deny you nothing for him.'

Ordination

Knowing that the road to secular preferment was barred by the King, Donne could only capitulate. Some lingering scruples remained, which he discussed with the King a few days later, when he agreed to accept ordination; and there were debts to be paid and other affairs to be put in order before he entered the church. But these last difficulties fell behind, and within two months of the meeting at Theobalds Donne was ordained deacon in the Anglican Church.

From this date until the end of his life in 1631 Donne enjoyed the growing distinction and material security which had eluded him throughout the frustrating years which followed his dismissal by Egerton. In 1616 he obtained two livings, in Huntingdonshire and

Kent, whose combined endowments gave him a comfortable income; and he was appointed to a well-paid post as preacher to the benchers of Lincoln's Inn. Five years later, in 1621, his fortunes were finally secured by his preferment as dean of St Paul's, which position he held until his death. But material success and the growing respect which came to Donne did not make this closing phase of his life entirely happy. In August 1617 his wife died, aged only thirty-three, a week after giving birth to another stillborn child. During their fifteen years of married life Ann had borne him twelve children, of whom seven had survived the considerable hazards of childhood. Walton, who generally seems concerned to make Donne's behaviour exemplary, tells how Donne promised his now motherless children that he would not marry again, and 'betook himself to most retired and solitary life'. A second wife might have eased his domestic problems and brought him some personal comfort, but Donne seems henceforward to have resigned himself to the bleakness of a life troubled and perhaps haunted by spiritual misgivings. The man who had regarded himself as enduring a long funeral during the empty years at Mitcham was not revived by the preferments which now came to him. So far as his poetry allows us to look into his personal feelings, it shows him threatened by increasing darkness of spirit.

Not all Donne's religious poetry was written after his ordination. One of the most striking of these poems is dated by its title, *Good Friday 1613, Riding Westward*. It is an interesting disclosure that at this time, when Donne was first expressing a wish to enter the Church and then trying to obtain the post of ambassador at Venice, he could write so heartfelt and contrite an appeal to God. His hankering after worldly distinction seems repeatedly to have collided with an equally powerful impulse towards self-abnegation and an austere religious discipline; rather as the opening lines of *Riding Westward* suggest, when Donne confesses that

> Pleasure or business so our souls admit
> For their First Mover, and are whirled by it:
> Hence is't that I am carried towards the west
> This day, when my soul's form bends toward the east.

The power of this wayward material interest makes it too strong to be mastered, and in several poems Donne appeals to God himself to discipline him by crushing the sinful impulse which alienates him from God's presence:

> O think me worth thine anger; punish me,
> Burn off my rusts and my deformity,
> Restore thine image so much, by thy grace,
> That thou mayst know me, and I'll turn my face.

Donne repeats this plea in a different form in *Holy Sonnet XIV*, where he calls upon God to break the knot that binds him to sin:

Take me to you, imprison me; for I,
Except you enthral me, never shall be free,
Nor ever chaste except you ravish me.

These two passages typify the pressure of Donne's need for an assurance which only divine intervention can bring him, taking possession of him with a violence matched by his own headlong energy of language. The intemperateness of his writing as a young man persists, though his object is no longer to overwhelm his mistress's objections but to compel God to acknowledge him. 'Swear by thyself', he insists in the closing stanza of his final poem, where the urgency of his fear nerves him to demand salvation,

that at my death thy sun
Shall shine as it shines now and heretofore.

The thought of the last day and its awesome judgment, which earlier had figured incongruously in several of the love poems, now becomes a haunting preoccupation which rises up to strike at Donne without warning. 'I dare not move my dim eyes any way,' he admits in *Holy Sonnet I*, which ends with another moving appeal to God;

Despair behind, and death before, doth cast
Such terror, and my feeble flesh doth waste
By sin in it, which it towards hell doth weigh.

Holy Sonnet XIII begins with a sudden burst of alarm as Donne recognizes that he may be called to his account before another sunrise: 'What if this present were the world's last night?' The self-assured lover of the *Songs and Sonets*, who basks in the certainty of achievement, has vanished completely, and has been replaced by a figure haggard with anxiety, whose yearning to be united with God is continually frustrated by the sins which he cannot expiate or forget.

What sin Donne had committed to be so oppressed he never reveals. His sense of indelible guilt was perhaps a product of the neurotic depression which troubled him throughout his life and which after the death of Ann Donne became increasingly severe. If he had indeed committed some moral crime, it is unlikely that the love poems give any reliable clue to its nature; and much more probable that Donne found it impossible to shake off the Catholic indoctrination that told him he was in a state of mortal sin. It seems to follow from this explanation that Donne's ministry as an Anglican priest was fundamentally insincere; but we should not assume that the issue was as simple for Donne as a plain choice between right and wrong. However strongly the buried impulse of his catholicism might protest against his decision, intellectually Donne must have argued himself into approval of the Anglican position. If he recognized any possibility that by taking orders under James he was sinning against the true Church, he might have felt that the sincerity of his dedication to God would weigh against this unwilling error. 'There are some things in which all religions agree,' he told his congregation a year before his death, the worship of God, the holiness of life. And therefore, if when I study this holiness of life, and fast and pray, and submit myself to discreet and medicinal mortifications for the subduing of my body, any man may say, 'This is papistical, papists do it', it is a blessed protestation; and no man is the less a protestant, nor the worse a protestant, for making it.

The quietly affirmative tone of this passage as well as its argument suggest that Donne had found the resolution of his private conflict in the belief that salvation could be reached through a direct relationship with God, not only through adherence to a single religion. Taken generally Donne's religious poems do not share this more assured mood. Rather, they reveal a degree of spiritual disturbance which only an upheaval as great as a renunciation of implanted faith might have caused.

Spiritual anxieties were not the only trouble which Donne had to contend with during this last phase of his life. His health had broken down several times during the years of privation at Mitcham, and was still precarious. In March 1619 he was appointed a member of an embassy sent to Germany in connection with the Bohemian succession, which threatened to bring Catholic rule into a hitherto protestant kingdom. Donne had no diplomatic training, and may have been sent out of England to find relief from overwork and persistent ill-health. 'I leave a scattered flock of wretched children,' he wrote to a friend before leaving for Germany, 'and I carry an infirm and valetudinary body.' To another friend he sent a copy of his poems and the manuscript of his unpublished treatise on suicide, *Biathanatos*, with the curious request that it should be neither printed nor burnt; asking that any other reader should be told when it had been composed, and that it was 'a book written by Jack Donne, and not by Dr Donne'.* Clearly he wished to be publicly dissociated from his younger self, though not to the extent that would involve destroying his earlier work. If he could not openly acknowledge Jack Donne, nor could he repudiate him entirely. Another backward glance to his youth is recorded in *A Hymn to Christ, at the Author's last going into Germany*, written before Donne embarked at Dover at the beginning of this journey. The tone of the poem suggests that Donne did not expect to return, and that he is concerned to set his house spiritually in order by renouncing all the remaining ties between himself and worldly affairs. 'Seal then this bill of my divorce', he tells God in conclusion,

> to all
> On whom those fainter beams of love did fall;
> Marry those loves which in youth scattered be
> On fame, wit, hopes—false mistresses—to thee.

These preparations were not yet needed. After being absent from the end of April 1619 until early January of the year following, Donne

*Donne was made an honorary D.D. of Cambridge in 1615, at the King's insistence.

returned to London 'with his sorrows moderated and his health improved': an improvement which seems to have encouraged a revival of his worldly ambitions. In 1621, learning that the deanery of Salisbury was to fall vacant, he interested himself in securing the post. From a letter written to the Duke of Buckingham in August that year, it appears that Donne had the promise of his support. 'Ever since I had your lordship's letter,' he remarks, 'I have esteemed myself in possession of Salisbury'; but the projected vacancy had not occurred, and Donne was left still wrestling with what he calls 'a narrow and penurious fortune'. The letter concludes with an abject appeal for Buckingham's favour which contrasts oddly, and perhaps disagreeably, with Donne's passionate longing to be seized by God. 'All that I mean in using this boldness,' he writes,

> of putting myself into your lordship's presence by this rag of paper, is to tell your lordship that I lie in a corner, as a clod of clay, attending what kind of vessel it shall please you to make of your lordship's humblest and thankfullest and devotedest servant.

His letter shows that Donne could prostrate himself in the cause of private ambition with much the same eagerness and self-abnegation as he expresses in his devotional writing, where he is prepared to regard himself as clay—'wet mud walls, that waste away faster than God meant at first they should'—without the hope of ingratiating himself with a great patron. This contradiction of purposes was too deeply embedded in Donne's nature to be simply explained. He seems to be two persons, worldly courtier and ascetic; on one hand compelling himself to adopt an unremitting spiritual discipline, and on the other still actively seeking material advancement as though the service of God were not enough. Later in the same year another opportunity of preferment occurred, when the dean of St Paul's was appointed bishop of Exeter; and again Donne's ambitions prompted him to approach Buckingham, whose closeness to the King made him a powerfully influential friend in the disposing of royal gifts. According to Walton's picturesque story, Donne was commanded to attend the King at dinner; and when James was at table he told him, before beginning to eat, that

> though you sit not down with me, yet I will carve to you of a dish which I know you love well; for knowing you love London, I do therefore make you dean of St Paul's; and when I have dined, then do you take your beloved dish home to your study, say grace there to yourself, and much good may it do you.

Donne was elected into his new office in November 1621. Three months later he found it necessary to resign his appointment as preacher to the benchers at Lincoln's Inn, but in his new circumstances this loss of income cannot have troubled him. Ill-health rather

S. PAULES CHURCH

the Water house

Quene hythe

Three Cranes

The Eell Schipes

The Gally fuste

THAMESIS

Old St Paul's, taken from Visscher's View of London, 1616.

than financial worries was the hazard which confronted him as he accepted the physical and nervous strains which fell upon him as dean of a great cathedral. In the autumn of 1623 he suffered a serious break-down of health, and became so dangerously ill that he was not ex-pected to survive. This illness, which lasted just over three weeks, allowed Donne's markedly introspective mind to pore over its most fascinating subject, studying and ruminating upon the changes of bodily and mental condition which succeeded one another as the sick-ness ran its course. The results of this unusual self-analysis were published early the following year as *Devotions upon emergent Occasions*, a prose work whose popularity led to three further editions within the next four years. Probably no other work of Donne's reveals him so clearly, or shows how strongly his outlook was coloured at this time by the idea of death. As a sick and possibly dying man he becomes, in his own macabre judgment, a symbolic figure, repesenting both the morally diseased state of man and the steadily worsening condition of the natural world. In the *First Anniversary* Donne had taken the death of Elizabeth Drury as an emblem by which 'the frailty and the decay of this whole world is represented'. Twelve years later he has himself be-come this ghastly emblematic figure; and he returns to his theme with the feverish interest of a man absorbed in the spectacle of his own approach to physical dissolution. 'Man, who is the noblest part of the earth,' he writes in Meditation II,

melts so away as if he were a statue not of earth but of snow. We see his own envy melts him, he grows lean with that; he will say an-other's beauty melts him. But he feels that a fever doth not melt him like snow but pour him out like lead, like iron, like brass melted in a furnace: it doth not only melt him but calcine him, reduce him to atoms and to ashes; not to water but to lime. And how quickly? Sooner than thou canst receive an answer, sooner than thou canst conceive the question.

In Meditation IV, repeating the familiar argument that man is a micro-cosm of the greater world he inhabits, he shows how both contain and breed evils which seek to destroy them.

As the other world produces serpents and vipers, malignant and venomous creatures, and worms and caterpillars, that endeavour to devour that world which produces them . . . so this world, our-selves, produces all these in us, in producing diseases and sicknesses of all those sorts: venomous and infectious diseases, feeding and consuming diseases, and manifold and entangled diseases made up of many several ones. And can the other world name so many veno-mous, so many consuming, so many monstrous creatures, as we can diseases of all these kinds?

The tolling of a bell for another man, less fortunate than himself, brings Donne to recognize in Meditation XVIII that he too must be considered dead. In the prayer which follows he revives the paradox of himself as a living corpse, an idea found in Donne's writing before he had considered entering the Church. 'That voice, that I must die now,' he recognizes as the bell tolls, 'is not the voice of a judge that speaks by way of condemnation, but of a physician that presents health in that. . . . I am dead, I was born dead; and from the first laying of these mud walls in my conception they have mouldered away, and the whole course of life is but an active death.'

In his morbid preoccupation with death and disease Donne takes on a symbolic character which he himself could not have perceived. An age was dying with him, and many of the most gifted writers of his time shared his neurotically depressed outlook. The elation and confidence of late sixteenth-century poetry—a spirit which Donne had caught in the masterful boldness of his early writing—waned and collapsed as the new century advanced, giving way to the melancholy foreboding which the tragedies of Webster express through their picture of a terrified and helpless humanity waiting to be struck down. For Donne, the macabre imaginings displayed in his *Devotions* were no new development. Several of the love poems startle the reader by introducing incongruous allusions to the lover's grave or his skeleton, to shrouds and corpses, and to the practice of disinterring bodies to make way for new burials. We may suppose that Donne used such images partly for their bizarre effect; but incongruity of this kind is native to him, and the interest in mortality which he wittily exploits in his early writing points ahead to the obsessive concern with death which dominates so many of his sermons. What seems an odd fancy in the love-poems has grown to envelop his mind, forcing him into a mesmerized contemplation of what both appals and fascinates him. 'Thou pursuest the works of the flesh, and hast none,' he argued in a sermon preached at Lincoln's Inn, 'for thy flesh is but dust held together by plasters. Dissolution and putrefaction is gone over thee alive: thou hast overlived thine own death, and art become thine own ghost and thine own hell.'

Argued and illustrated again and again, this obsession with physical decay and the dissolution of the body pursued Donne to the end of his final sermon, delivered shortly before his death in 1631 and published as *Death's Duel* shortly afterwards. 'For us that die now, and sleep in the state of the dead,' he told his congregation,

we must all pass this posthume death, this death after death, nay, this death after burial, this dissolution after dissolution; this death of corruption and putrefaction, of vermiculation and incineration, of dissolution and dispersion in and from the grave. . . This is the most inglorious and contemptible vilification, the most deadly and peremptory nullification of man, that we can consider.

Title-page of Dekker's A Rod For Runaways, *1625.*

A Rod *for* Run-awayes.

which flight oftheirs, if they looke backe, they may
behold many fearefull Iudgements of God, fundry wayes pronounced vpon this City, and on feuerall perfons, both
flying from it, and ftaying in it.

xprefsed in many dreadfull Examples of fudden Death, falne vpon both young and
old, within this City, and the Suburbes, in the Fields, and open Streets, to the
terrour of all thofe who liue, and to the warning of thofe who are to
dye, to be ready when God Almighty fhall bee pleafed
to call them.

With additions of fome new Accidents.

Written by T H O. D.

Lord, haue mercy   on London.

I follow.   We fly

Wee dye.   Keepe out

nted at London for *Iohn Trundle*, and are to be fold at his Shop in Smithfield. 1625.

The shadow of the shroud

During the closing years of Donne's life his health deteriorated steadily. Repeated attacks of fever left him emaciated and wasted, as though to illustrate the paradoxical view which Donne had taken of himself as a man long dead who had become his own ghost. He survived the major epidemic of plague which swept London in 1625 and almost halted the life of the city, by taking refuge in Chelsea with Sir John and Lady Danvers. There, in the household of the old friend whom he had previously known as Magdalen Herbert, he spent the summer revising and preparing many of his sermons—a letter mentions eighty of them—for publication; and he may have written *The Autumnal* as an unconventional poetic tribute to his hostess. The plague followed Donne to Chelsea, but he was not to join the thousands of Londoners buried every week as the disease ravaged a terrified city. Donne's end was to take a form poetically appropriate to the prolonged conflict of mind and spirit which had exhausted his once vigorous energy and self-confidence: that of a man reduced to the shell of himself, whose life had been a long funeral preparation for the final act of dying. Two further serious breakdowns of health, in 1628 and 1629, left him unable to carry out his duties for several months. He was unable to preach in St Paul's on Christmas Day 1629, and during the winter following illness again prevented him from preaching before the King at Christmas. In December 1630, recognizing that he might not have much longer to live, he made his will; a document which throws some interesting light on Donne's personal tastes and acquisitions.

Its unexpected disclosure is that Donne had been something of a collector of paintings, four of which he left to his executor Henry King. A picture of Adam and Eve, another of the Virgin Mary, and a Deposition of Christ form three more bequests. Another close acquaintance was to receive his painting of Mary Magdalen; and to the dean of Gloucester Donne bequeathed 'the picture called the Skeleton which hangs in the hall', presumably a *memento mori*. The old friend who had put himself in jeopardy nearly thirty years earlier by marrying Donne to Ann More was remembered by the gift of 'the picture of the Blessed Virgin and Joseph which hangs in my study', while four large pictures 'of the four great prophets' were to remain in the deanery. Several other paintings to be chosen by Donne's beneficiaries are not identified by subject, but the last to be mentioned is described in terms which must arouse interest. To Robert Ker, his friend and correspondent for many years, Donne bequeathed 'that picture of mine which is taken in shadows and was made very many years before I was of this profession'. This must be a portrait of Donne, unusual in showing the sitter 'in shadows' instead of evenly lit, as was the Elizabethan custom. The remark about its being painted 'very many years' previously seems to imply that Donne wished to disclaim his connection with this younger self. The portrait may

Engraving of Donne in a shroud, prefaced to Death's Duel, *1632.*

EFFIGIES REVERENDISSIMI VIRI JOHANNIS DONNE NUPER ECCLESIÆ CATHEDRALIS DECANI.

Corporis hæc Animæ sit Syndon, Syndon Jesu
Amen.

artin ᴅ scup. And are to be sould by R R and Ben: ffisher

have depicted him as an arrogant man of fashion, extravagantly dressed; or it may have hinted too clearly for Donne's later comfort at the wildness which he had outgrown. By the end of his life all physical traces of the fiery young man whom he had been were obliterated, and Donne had purposefully shaped himself into the grim and self-mocking image which he intended to bequeath to St Paul's: an effigy of his own corpse, made ready for the burial which he felt had been so long delayed.

Walton relates how Donne's final portrait was painted, in the costume and posture appropriate to the identity which Donne was about to take over in earnest. He obtained a wooden urn, large enough for him to stand on, and then dressed himself in his winding-sheet,

so tied with knots at his head and feet, and his hands so placed, as dead bodies are usually fitted to be shrouded and put into their coffin or grave. Upon this urn he stood with his eyes shut, and with so much of the sheet turned aside as might show his lean, pale and deathlike face, which was purposely turned toward the east, from whence he expected the second coming of our Saviour.

The full-length portrait was then placed at Donne's bedside, 'where it continued and became his hourly object till his death'. It is not mentioned in Donne's will, but Walton records that it passed into the hands of Henry King, who commissioned the effigy in white marble which was executed from the portrait by Nicholas Stone, the most eminent sculptor of the time. The effigy was then set up in St Paul's, where it still stands, virtually undamaged by the Great Fire which destroyed almost every other trace of the medieval cathedral known to Donne. The lucky chance which spared this monument enables us to bring a study of Donne's personal life to an end on perhaps the most revealing indication of his inner self which he left to the world. When Walton mentions that he has seen 'many pictures of him, in several habits, and at several ages and in several postures' we are not surprised. Donne never escaped from himself, or broke loose from the introspective habit which made him probe and question the workings of his own mind and spirit. His evident fondness for having his portrait painted at every stage of life is not an admission of vanity, but another mark of the tireless curiosity about himself which is most openly declared in his *Devotions*. So persistent a desire to see himself objectively represented and shown to exist might have been impelled by a private fear in Donne that he had no real exist-ence: that he had already been annihilated, and was nothing. Such a suggestion is in fact made in some of the love poems, where Donne argues that absence 'withdrew our souls, and made us carcasses', and that he and his mistress 'are nothing then, when on a divers shore'.

It would be wrong to regard such remarks as merely playful. Suitably amended, they reappear in his devotional writing when Donne expresses an agonized fear that God may reject him, 'let my soul fall out of his hand into a bottomless pit, and roll an unremovable stone upon it, and leave it to that which it finds there . . . and never think more of that soul, never have more to do with it.'

The fear of desertion which preyed upon Donne's mind could never be completely silenced; yet for the man who had encouraged himself to think of himself as a corpse awaiting burial the prospect of physical annihilation, that 'most deadly and peremptory nullification of man', cannot have been entirely unattractive. As a dead man, perhaps, he would possess the positive reality which had eluded him in his search for the substantial identity of John Donne. He was so far from fearing death in his last illness, Donne told his physician, 'which to others is the king of terrors, that he longed for the day of his dissolution'. Death had been the king of terrors for Donne too; but the dead were beyond reach of such fears. 'We die every day, and we die all the day long,' he had told his congregation ten years previously, 'and because we are not absolutely dead we call that an eternity, an eternity of dying: and is there comfort in that state? Why, it is the state of hell itself; eternal dying, and not dead.'

The portraits 'in several habits and in several postures' known to Walton represented Donne's lifelong attempt to externalize himself as a living reality, and to break away from the conviction that he was at best a creature 'not absolutely dead'. But the conviction proved irresistible. By the end of his life it so far dominated his mind that the only image which he could willingly leave to posterity was the corpse-like figure within the knotted shroud which still perpetuates him, in Donne's last and most paradoxical attempt to portray himself.

Critical reputation

Donne's reputation as a poet, and his influence on other writers, were chiefly posthumous. His sermons made him famous and respected throughout the city, while his poetry was a private occupation, little known outside the circle of friends and fellow-writers who saw his work in manuscript. If we can believe Jonson, these copies of Donne's poems may have been harder to come by after his ordination, for 'now since he was made doctor [he] repenteth highly and seeketh to destroy all his poems'. Donne's divided feelings towards *Biathanatos*, which was neither to be published nor burnt, make it seem unlikely that he wished to destroy any of his writing; though as priest he might well have felt anxious that his love poems should not come into the wrong hands. He was spared any such scandal. The poems were first published in 1633, two years after his death. Two further editions appeared in 1635 and 1639, in which the poems were divided into the groups familiar to modern readers—*Songs and Sonets**, *Elegies, Satires, Letters, Divine Poems* and some lesser categories. Evidently Donne's family was not consulted by his anonymous editor, and it is clear that no permission to publish the poems had been given. In 1637 the younger John Donne petitioned the Archbishop of Canterbury to forbid the printing and publishing of the 'many scandalous pamphlets' issued under his father's name since Donne's death, speaking as though these works were entirely spurious. The list includes the poems, published 'very much to the grief of your petitioner, and the discredit of the memory of his father': a comment which does not specifically deny that the poems were Donne's, but which shows how unwelcome the disclosure of his youthful character had been to his family.

The reputation which Donne's son thought in danger was solidly upheld in 1640, when the great folio collection of eighty sermons was published. The son could not have known that the most authoritative critic of the age had acknowledged Donne 'the first poet in the world in some things'; and presumably he was unimpressed by the tributes from Donne's fellow-poets printed as a preface to the collected poems. The best known of these was contributed by Carew, who generously admits Donne's originality and inventiveness:

> The Muses' garden, with pedantic weeds
> O'erspread, was purged by thee: the lazy seeds
> Of servile imitation thrown away,
> And fresh invention planted. Thou didst pay
> The debts of our penurious bankrupt age.

His praise of Donne is more than uncritical eulogy. Carew recognizes that his style is generally rough and unmusical, and argues that Donne deserves credit for turning the stiffness and inflexibility of English to his advantage:

> Thou mayst claim
> From so great disadvantage greater fame,
> Since to the awe of thy imperious wit
> Our stubborn language bends, made only fit
> With her tough thick-ribbed hoops to gird about
> Thy giant fancy, which had proved too stout
> For their soft melting phrases.

But although Donne's inventive wit appealed strongly to the gentleman poets of this time, Jonson's insistence upon clarity and natural expression stood against any inclination they may have felt to imitate the sometimes brutal forcing of language to which Carew refers. The damning remark that Donne, 'for not keeping of accent, deserved

---

*Sonets, as distinct from sonnets, are described as short poems or pieces of verse. The title misrepresents the character of Donne's love-poems by suggesting a predominantly lyrical tone.

hanging', implies that Jonson misunderstood one of the most important characteristics of Donne's poetry: its substitution of colloquial speech rhythms for the regular metrical patterns which most Elizabethan poets had adopted. Seen from the viewpoint of conventional writing, Donne's poetry often contained more syllables, stressed words, caesuras and other metrical irregularities than the lines seemed able to contain without losing rhythmical pattern altogether. But Donne had not tried to write regular verse. His rhythms are continually shifting and varying as he follows the accents of the speaking voice, now rapid with impatience, now dragging with resignation; twisting and misshaping language structure as he compels words to accept his argument, as though against their will. The result is one of the most strikingly individual forms of expression contrived by a poet: a style which justifies itself by representing the poet's struggle to realize curiously involved ideas within the framework of a literary form, and one which could not be imitated.

During the second quarter of the seventeenth century there were few English poets who resisted Donne's influence as the master of witty contrast and analogy. As he had represented the relationship of parted lovers by an image of compasses, so Lovelace could describe a lady's glove as a farm with five tenements, and Marvell a glow-worm as a country comet. But their quaint and consciously mannered images were set in poems that were rhythmically smooth and regular; and the roughness that came from Donne's wrestling with words was imitated only by a few later satirists, who believed that abusive writing should be metrically discordant. The important difference between Donne and the most prominent of these imitators was neatly defined by Dryden. 'We cannot read a verse of Cleveland's without making a face at it,' he wrote in 1668, 'as if every work were a pill to swallow: he gives us many times a hard nut to break our teeth, without a kernel for our pains. So that there is this difference betwixt his satires and Dr Donne's; that the one gives us deep thoughts in common language, though rough cadence; the other gives us common thoughts in abstruse words.'

But although at this date Dryden could give his approval to the roughness of Donne's style, twenty-five years later the change in literary taste towards urbanity and correctness led him to take a different attitude towards the same subject. 'Would not Donne's Satires,' he asked, 'which abound with so much wit, appear more charming if he had taken care of his words and of his numbers?' He seems to have adopted Jonson's unsympathetic view of Donne's unevenly stressed lines, and to have lost his respect for what he had previously called 'deep thoughts'. Dryden now complains that Donne 'affects the metaphysics, not only in his satires but in his amorous verses, where nature only should reign; and perplexes the minds of the fair sex with nice speculations of philosophy, when he should engage their hearts and entertain them with the softnesses of love'.

This passage is remembered chiefly for its association of Donne's poetry with metaphysical ideas, which Dryden was first to make;* but we should also notice its rejection of speculative argument as a fitting subject of poetry. New literary standards were beginning to crystallize, and wit was soon to be defined as the expressing of familiar ideas in new and elegant form: a criterion which Donne's startling originality of thought and uncouth energy could not satisfy. One eminent eighteenth-century critic dismissed Donne's poetry as 'nothing but a continued heap of riddles', and Pope complained that his style was 'rugged and most unmusical'; though he recognized that Donne's language had not become out of date. The objections which eighteenth-century readers felt towards metaphysical poetry were summed up when Dr Johnson wrote a critical essay on Cowley in his *Lives of the Poets*, published in 1778. Cowley, who flourished a generation after the death of Donne, is not much regarded by modern critics, and it says a good deal for the general lack of appreciation which Donne's poetry suffered that Cowley's timid manipulation of metaphysical stock-in-trade should have been preferred to the inventive vigour of Donne.

Johnson's critical strictures are directed at metaphysical poetry in general, and he does not often refer to Donne in particular but assumes that the same complaints can be made of him as of Cleveland and Cowley. Few modern readers would agree; but it is interesting to see how Donne appeared to this great eighteenth-century conservative. 'The metaphysical poets were men of learning,' Johnson remarks, 'and to show their learning was their whole endeavour.' This may be true of Donne's imitators, who delighted to find bizarre analogies between common experience and bookish ideas—Marvell sees the mowers as Israelites passing through the green sea of the meadow—but Donne does not simply put his learning on show. His allusions to science and Scholastic philosophy are brought in not to decorate his poems, but as part of the argument which is their *raison d'être*. When Johnson asserted that the metaphysical poets 'neither copied nature nor life, neither painted the forms of matter, nor represented the operations of intellect', he was only partly right; for although Donne never describes his mistress and ignores the natural world almost completely, his poems represent the process of thought by which Donne moves towards an intellectual goal. But Johnson evidently found it difficult to distinguish between the genuine oddity of Donne's thinking and the consciously fantastic style which later poets developed from his example. 'Their thoughts are often new, but seldom natural', Johnson complained, including Donne with his imitators,

*Metaphysics is defined as a branch of speculative enquiry dealing with such concepts as being, substance, time, identity and so on. More commonly, it is taken to be the study of abstract and immaterial things, like the angels whose nature Donne discusses in *Air and Angels*. Not many of his poems justify Dryden's use of the term 'metaphysics' in this way.

they are not obvious, but neither are they just; and the reader, far from wondering that he missed them, wonders more frequently by what perverseness of industry they were ever found . . . The most heterogeneous ideas are yoked by violence together; nature and art are ransacked for illustrations, comparisons and allusions.

The main task of poetry, Johnson believed, was to renew the appeal and interest of ideas which every generation rediscovered; and he criticized the metaphysical poets for searching so much after intellectual novelty and surprise that they lost touch with common truth. 'Great thoughts are always general,' he insisted, certain that fondness for the unusual could only produce trivial ideas. Those writers who lay in watch for novelty, he argued, 'could have little hope of greatness, for great things cannot have escaped former observation'. This disposed of Donne's originality, but Johnson's prejudices did not prevent him from appreciating that despite their mistaken respect for the odd and the fanciful, the metaphysical poets sometimes produced arresting ideas. If they frequently threw away their wit upon false conceits, he conceded, 'they likewise sometimes struck out unexpected truth. If their conceits were far-fetched, they were often worth the carriage. To write on their plan, it was at least necessary to read and think.' This just comment will seem more generous in a critic of Johnson's time when we remember that he is speaking more particularly of Cowley than of Donne; but although we must respect the critical honesty of this admission, we should probably not wish to praise metaphysical poetry for its 'unexpected truth'. Unlike Johnson, a modern reader does not look for instruction from poetry: he expects to share an experience which the poet causes to happen by releasing the energies of language. But this was not an aspect of Donne's poetry which an eighteenth-century critic was likely to praise, had he recognized it.

Johnson's essay helped to fasten the description 'metaphysical' more firmly to this group of poets, despite its inappropriateness. When De Quincey protested against the title in 1828 it was too late to resist what had become settled practice. 'Metaphysical they were not', De Quincey wrote; 'Rhetorical would have been a more accurate designation.' He went on to explain that he was using the term in its original sense, 'as laying the principal stress upon the management of the thoughts, and only a secondary one upon the ornaments of style'. This hints at a clearer understanding of Donne's purpose than any previous critic had shown; and the comment which followed shows still more critical perception: 'Few writers have shown a more extraordinary compass of powers than Donne; for he combined—what no other man has done—the last sublimation of dialectical subtlety and address with the most impassioned majesty.' But for De Quincey as for earlier commentators, the colloquial rhythms of Donne's verse were still so far from being heard that he could complain of the 'intolerable defect of ear' that marred

Donne's poetry. His misunderstanding was widely shared by other nineteenth-century writers, who must either have missed or disregarded a remark made by Coleridge and published in the *Lectures* of 1818. To read Dryden or Pope, Coleridge pointed out, 'you need only count syllables; but to read Donne you must measure *time*, and discover the time of each word by the sense of passion. . . . Not one in a thousand of his readers has any notion how his lines are to be read—to the many, five out of six appear anti-metrical.' Wordsworth confirms the impression that Donne was generally undervalued or ignored at this time, when after praising *Holy Sonnet X* he admits that 'to modern taste it may be repulsive, quaint and laboured'. A little later, in 1839, Tennyson's friend Hallam went much further in a sweeping condemnation of Donne's poetry, which he found uncouth and unintelligible; and allowed himself a disapproving sniff directed towards the love poems:

> Donne is the most inharmonious of our versifiers, if he can be said to have deserved such a name by lines too rugged to seem metre. Of his earlier poems many are very licentious; the latter are chiefly devout. Few are good for much; the conceits have not even the merit of being intelligible; it would perhaps be difficult to select three passages that we should care to read again.

But not all Victorian poets were ready to dismiss Donne as abruptly as this. Browning and Swinburne both admired him, and towards the end of the nineteenth century the critic Edward Dowden suggested that some of the difficulties confronting the reader of Donne could be removed by appreciating the literary traditions of his age. Dowden was not prepared to recognize Donne as the founder of a school of English poetry. 'I do not believe in the existence of this so-called "metaphysical school"', he wrote; and he pointed out that a delight in subtleties of thought, ingenuity and fantastic ideas is characteristic of Elizabethan writing. This was a timely observation, for hitherto Donne had been regarded as a poet who broke away from the central tradition represented by Shakespeare to develop a new literary interest. Donne was coming to be recognized both as a typical Elizabethan in the extravagance of his wit, and as a poet whose work was to be judged not by the irrelevant criterion of metrical form but by its passionate feeling.

Writing in 1896, George Saintsbury felt obliged to admit that 'no one with the finest sense of poetry as an art could have left things so formless' as some of Donne's poems; but he asserted that for the reader who knew something of human passion 'there is no poet and hardly any writer like Donne'. This great change in critical attitude made it possible for Saintsbury to see what earlier commentators had hidden from themselves by supposing that the irregularity of Donne's verse was inadvertent: that his style might be 'an index and reflection of the variety and rapid changes of his thought and feeling'. What had been mistaken for clumsiness and insensitivity was Donne's means of indicating the growth of excited feeling, by varying stress and movement to match the fluctuating emotions behind the argument. Unlike Dryden, who had rebuked Donne for perplexing his mistress with philosophical talk, Saintsbury perceived that these seemingly detached arguments were driven by a passionate energy which Donne never describes, but represents through the irregular movement of his verse. In a picturesque analogy, Saintsbury admitted that this passionate energy was not always able to master the intellectual concepts which Donne heaped upon it. 'But the fire is always there,' he went on, 'overtasked, overmastered for a time, but never choked or extinguished; and ever and anon from gaps in the smouldering mass there breaks forth such a sudden flow of pure molten metal, such a flower of incandescence, as not even in the very greatest poets of all can be ever surpassed.' Admiration of Donne was now moving his critics to rapture. Four years later Sir Walter Raleigh defended the poet against another familiar charge by asserting that there was little extravagance in Donne's conceits: 'The vast overshadowing canopy of his imagination seems to bring the most wildly dissimilar things together with ease.'

In 1899 Edmund Gosse produced a biography of Donne in two volumes which included many long extracts from the poet's letters. Although Gosse assumed without right that the poems could be used as biographical material, his picture of Donne's life was a helpful adjunct to the literary work, and a means of widening the common appreciation of Donne. Then in 1912, when Herbert Grierson's edition of the poems was published with a full critical apparatus, Donne at last received the accolade of scholarly recognition. After this milestone, the last important contribution to the understanding of Donne that need be mentioned here was made in 1921, in the now famous essay by T. S. Eliot which appeared under the title, 'The Metaphysical Poets'. Like some of his predecessors, Eliot was disposed to question the appropriateness of this term, though for reasons very much his own. He recognized no intellectual bias in Donne's poetry, and insisted that, to the contrary, Donne and some of his contemporaries were men who 'incorporated their erudition into their sensibility: their mode of feeling was directly and freshly altered by their reading and thought'. Where other critics had found bare dialectical argument, Eliot saw a fusion of thought and feeling: in his own words, 'a direct sensuous apprehension of thought, or a re-creation of thought into feeling'. In a passage of his essay now perhaps better known than any other critical comment on metaphysical poetry he explained:

When a poet's mind is perfectly equipped for its work, it is constantly amalgamating disparate experience; the ordinary man's experience is chaotic, irregular, fragmentary. The latter falls in love, or reads Spinoza, and these two experiences have nothing to do with each other, or with the noise of the typewriter or the smell of cooking; in the mind of the poet these experiences are always forming new wholes.

This ability to combine disparate kinds of experience, Eliot believed, was especially marked in poets of the early seventeenth century, who possessed 'a mechanism of sensibility which could devour any kind of experience'. Their importance for Eliot was increased by what he called a 'dissociation of sensibility' as the combined influence of Milton and Dryden came to bear upon English poetry. Language became more refined, while feeling became cruder; and later poets had been unable to recover the power of fusing the two elements of experience in what Eliot called a direct sensuous apprehension of thought. His theory of the dissociation of sensibility, at first widely accepted, had lost most of its appeal by the middle of this century, but it had served a valuable purpose by stimulating a fresh appraisal of Donne's achievement and a new approach to the poetry of his age. It was largely in consequence of his own critical reassessment of Donne that Eliot could affirm in 1931 that Donne's literary standing had been permanently improved. His merit, Eliot observed in his summing-up, was to have substituted a natural conversational idiom for a conventional one, carrying out a revolution of the kind 'which has to occur from time to time . . . if the English language is to retain its vigour'.

2 The religious background

The Elizabethan settlement

In respect of religious affairs, the reign of Elizabeth was an unquiet age. For this the Queen was hardly to blame. She inherited a kingdom whose religious traditions had already been seriously disturbed, and constitutional wisdom required her to steer a course between extremes of faith, in an attempt to bring as many of her subjects as possible within a new communion—that of the Anglican Church. The disturbance of established religion had its beginnings twenty-five years before her accession, when her father Henry VIII set himself against the authority of the Pope and declared himself head of an independent Church of England. There was no sudden disappearance of Roman Catholic ritual and practice, for the king had no sympathy with the Protestant movement initiated by Luther in Germany; but there was some modification of Catholic doctrine, the clergy was enjoined to preach sermons, and an authorized translation of the Bible was published in 1535. Such changes, with the destruction or removal of images, the dissolution of the monastic houses and the desecration of religious shrines, transformed the appearance of English Catholic life; and by making the scriptures accessible to the unlearned, and cutting away much that was inessential to faith, these changes tended towards the simplicity and self-reliance of Protestantism. On the other hand, when an order was issued for the celebration of communion, as distinct from mass, the statute disclaimed any intention of condemning other forms of the same rite; and mass was not immediately rejected. The new Prayer Book published in 1548 was a compromise between the traditional and the reformed, though entirely in English. Under the guidance of Cranmer, the new Church was steadily feeling its way towards a version of modified catholicism, tempered to the outlook of a people who had grown resentful of alien authority and inclined towards a simple form of religious expression.

The wish for change was not universal, but the power of the crown working through the archbishops who were no longer appointed by the Pope would probably have assured the eventual establishment of Anglo-catholicism without any great protest. The hope of peaceful transformation was lost in 1553, when the shortlived Edward VI was succeeded by his half-sister Mary I, an ardent Catholic. Acknowledging the authority of the Pope, Mary reunited her kingdom with the Catholic world from which her father had separated it, annulled all the changes and reformations brought about in the previous twenty years, and began a persecution of her Protestant subjects which did more to injure her cause than had their heresies. Before her death in 1558 some three hundred English men and women were burnt at the stake as martyrs to their faith, as Mary attempted vainly to stamp out the religion which had been taking shape since the Reformation. The memory of this savage persecution was to remain in the popular mind throughout the reign of Elizabeth, causing catholicism to be feared and hated by the great body of her subjects who regarded themselves as members of the English Church. Any hope of reconciling the conflicting outlooks of Catholic and Protestant within a single communion was now lost, as each side adopted a fiercely dogmatic position which could only be satisfied by complete victory over the other.

Unlike her half-sister Mary, Elizabeth* had no strong religious persuasion; and did not act as though she felt obliged to impose religious belief upon her subjects. Throughout her reign, she and her ministers showed more concern for the political unity and stability of the realm than for religious dogma, of whatever form; and at different times the religious extremists among her people, whether Protestant or Catholic, were treated with the same severity. Evidently she was prepared to be tolerant and to allow differences of private faith, so long as there was outward conformity with the established religion and no attempt to challenge her authority as head of the English Church. But many of her subjects could not accept such a compromise. Those who were Catholics were bound by their faith to recognize the supreme authority of the Pope, and could not subscribe to the principles of another faith without committing heinous sin. On the other side the Protestant extremists, many of whom had gone into exile during the Marian persecution, were noisily discontented with the moderateness of the ecclesiastical reforms carried out under the Queen. Exile had brought them into contact with Calvinism, a doctrine which appealed strongly to the general disposition of Protestants to reduce the outward forms of religion to a bare minimum, and to regard the Bible rather than the priest as the mouthpiece of God's purposes.

In their clamour for still greater reforms within the English Church, and in their disrespect for Elizabeth's bishops and clergy, these Puritans—to give them their distinguishing title—were as great a cause of unrest and anxiety to the Elizabethan establishment as the Catholics, whose loyalty to the crown could never be wholehearted. Thus although Elizabeth might have preferred to allow her subjects a measure of religious freedom, as political ruler she could not afford to be tolerant. However dissimilar in other respects, Catholic and Puritan were alike in believing it their mission to overthrow the established faith, and to replace it by a form of religious extremism such as England had suffered under Mary. Simple political expediency, to say nothing of self-preservation, made it inevitable that Elizabeth should herself accept some degree of religious persecution and repression for the sake of stable government.

*Mary was the daughter of Henry VIII's first Queen, Catherine of Aragon; Elizabeth the daughter of her successor, Anne Boleyn.

She began her reign by returning to the position taken up by Henry VIII. By the Act of Supremacy, which became law in 1559, the Queen was declared supreme head of the Church as her father had been; his anti-papal statutes were revived, and the reactionary laws passed under Mary were annulled. The Anglican prayer book was restored to use in churches throughout the country, and clergy who refused to comply with the order were made liable to fines and imprisonment. More stringent forms of punishment were reserved for those who refused to take the oath of supremacy, or who declared that any foreign prince, prelate or potentate had authority within the Queen's realm. This clause was directed principally against the Catholic contention that the Pope remained head of the English Church; and the oath had the effect of barring professional life to all sincere Catholics. It was to be sworn by all clergy, judges, mayors, and royal officials; and also by those receiving university degrees and religious orders. Since it involved denying the authority of the Pope, the educated Catholics in Elizabethan England were forced to decide between abjuring their faith or forgoing qualifications or preferment within their chosen calling.

The Act of Supremacy began to bite as soon as it was put into force. All the bishops but one refused to take the oath, and were deprived of office; but the parish priests installed under Mary ignored this example, and with only few exceptions they adapted themselves to the new regime. Their compliance with the Act was an encouragement to their congregations to follow this lead. We should remember that however different the form of divine service under Elizabeth, it was celebrated in the same parish churches as the Catholic worshipper had attended under Mary; and that to continue an old habit was easier than to turn aside to a service held in secret by a Catholic priest. Those who refused to attend Anglican services for reasons of conscience were fined as recusants, and later were likely to be questioned about their loyalty. It seems probable that most Catholics neither embraced the new faith nor abandoned the old, but contrived an uneasy compromise between their duty as loyal subjects of the Queen and their spiritual obligations; joining both in the communion and in the mass. The state encouraged such equivocal behaviour by not enquiring into the private belief of the individual, and by being satisfied if there was outward conformity.

Catholic recusants

The new Church was given a settled body of doctrine in 1571, when parliament sanctioned the Thirty-nine Articles which had been drawn up eight years earlier. The delay was due to the Queen's refusal to allow parliament to introduce a bill affecting religion, which she held to be a matter for her own prerogative as head of the established Church. The same objection was to frustrate attempts by Puritans to introduce further religious reforms later in the reign, where again the Queen held up changes that many of her subjects would have resented. However, in 1570 an event occurred which made it impossible for Elizabeth to continue the policy of giving a broad measure of religious tolerance to the Catholic recusants. In February 1570 the Pope passed a sentence of excommunication upon the Queen, declaring her a pretended ruler and deposing her forthwith. The intention of this papal bull, which was surreptitiously published in London three months later, was to make it impossible for English Catholics—who were believed in Rome to be ready to rise against her—to continue to behave as loyal subjects of the crown. After 1570, those who obeyed the Queen's laws and respected her authority put themselves in hazard of the same sentence of excommunication. The compromise adopted by most Catholics, which admitted loyalty both to the Queen as political head and to the Pope as religious authority, was now ruled out; and it became the duty of the English recusants to seek the downfall of Elizabeth and her ministers. In fact the Queen was in no great danger. Only shortly before the Pope's sentence she had put down a rising in the north of England, where recusancy was strongest; and by suppressing this rebellion she had disabled those who were most likely to have rebelled against their excommunicated ruler. The common people seem to have been unimpressed by the Pope's action, and an outburst of scurrilous pamphlets ridiculed his presumption, 'as if no prince in the world might rule without his sufferance'. None the less his bull had brought the Queen and her government into a hazard which could not be ignored, especially when it was seen that recusancy increased and hardened in consequence of the papal decree. Further measures against the Catholics followed inevitably.

If the Pope's sentence against Elizabeth was to be made effective, the Queen would have to be deposed by force; either by armed rebellion or by foreign invasion. When the threat of invasion came to a head in 1588, it was met by a nation united behind their Queen; and the destruction of the Spanish armada was received as proof of God's support of the Protestant cause. After this decisive repulse of a would-be invader the danger of foreign intervention could be discounted, but Elizabeth continued to be troubled by the activities of Catholic seminarists, or trained missionaries, who risked death by defying her edicts. Shortly before the papal pronouncement against Elizabeth, a college had been set up at Douai in northern France to provide education for the families of English Catholics who had gone into exile for conscience' sake. This scheme proved so successful that its purposes were soon extended to the training of young men for the fight against Protestantism and the re-establishment of the old faith in England. Despite Elizabeth's attempts to prevent young Catholics from going abroad to join this seminary, they left England in such numbers that similar colleges were instituted at Rome, Valladolid and Seville to accommodate them.*

These seminarists submitted themselves to seven years' rigorous training of mind and body, pledging themselves to receive holy orders and to return to England 'for the salvation of souls' whenever the superior of the college directed. The fact that their activities were treasonable cannot blind us to their courage and religious devotion, for Elizabeth's secret service was constantly on the watch for seminary priests, who could expect the most horrible of deaths if they were captured. But we have also to recognize that their undoubted concern with the salvation of souls necessarily involved them in political subversion. By strengthening the Catholic cause in England, they were siding with the authority which had excommunicated and deposed the Queen; and even had these missionaries wished to confine themselves to pastoral duties, they were nourishing a force which would, if it became strong enough, overthrow not merely the English Church but the political establishment. Their presence in the country— at least a hundred of them had returned to England by 1580—constituted a more dangerous threat to the safety of Elizabeth's realm than the prospect of military invasion, and she took up the challenge savagely.

Elizabeth's persecution of the Catholics in the years following 1580 may seem better justified when we learn that by this date the new Pope had gone well beyond his predecessor's measures against Elizabeth. Not only had he encouraged plans of invading England through Ireland or the Low Countries, but he had discreetly published his opinion that the assassination of Elizabeth in the cause of religion could not be held a sin. By advocating regicide to the English Catholics he gave the Queen the best of reasons for sharpening the penalties which she had already imposed for recusancy. The fine for non-attendance at Sunday service, hitherto fixed at a shilling, was increased to the huge sum of £20 per month; and the offender was obliged to find a further £200 as security for his future compliance with the act.†
If a recusant was unable to pay the fine, the crown was entitled to seize all his goods and two-thirds of his land and other property. For saying or singing mass a fine of two hundred marks—about £125—was now to be levied, and the offender to be imprisoned for a year; and each member of such a congregation was to pay a hundred marks' fine and suffer the same term of imprisonment. Any Catholic priest who attempted to make converts from those of the established faith made himself guilty of treason, a capital offence. All seminary priests and Jesuits were ordered to leave the country on pain of death, and those of the Queen's subjects studying in foreign seminaries were ordered to return to England and to prove their loyalty by taking the

*We cannot suppose that all English Catholics approved and supported the activities of the seminarists. Many of the gentry hoped to find a compromise between their religious obligations to Rome and their patriotic feelings as subjects of the English queen.

†To appreciate the value of Elizabethan money, we might remember that Shakespeare paid £60 for his house at Stratford-on-Avon.

oath of supremacy; in default of which they would be declared traitors. Suspected priests who refused to answer a judge's interrogation might be held in prison indefinitely; and to check the movement of recusants about the realm such persons were ordered not to travel more than five miles from their homes, on pain of forfeiting all their property. Those who uttered slanderous or seditious rumours about the Queen were to be set in the pillory, to lose both ears and to be fined £200; and the publishing of seditious books was made a felony punishable by death.

The severity of these anti-Catholic laws, and the ghastly apparatus of torture and lingering death which awaited many of their victims, suggests that the persecution of the Catholics under Elizabeth grew to be as brutal and inhumane as Mary's attempts to stamp out protestantism thirty years earlier. In defence of Elizabeth it can be argued that where some two hundred and fifty Catholics were martyred for their faith during twenty years of her reign, Mary had sent three hundred protestants to the stake in five years; but the greater horror of the Marian persecution should not encourage us to see Elizabeth's behaviour as humane and enlightened. By accepting the rack, the pillory and the disembowelling-knife as instruments of policy she called the moral right of her government into question, and gave her enemies some apparent justification for seeking her overthrow. But a Catholic successor would have been obliged to use the same instruments of persecution and terror to break the will of Protestant England, and to bring its Church again under the rule of the Pope. At a time when Spain was known to be preparing an armada against England, and when every English Catholic was obliged by his faith to regard the Queen as a desposed heretic, it is hard to see that Elizabeth could have acted otherwise. Her mildness towards the old religion at the beginning of her reign, and her obvious hope that Catholics would adopt a compromise of conscience as loyal subjects, shows that unlike Mary she had no wish to make private faith a matter for persecution; but as a ruler with the material interests of her subjects at heart she could only resist the determined attempts of a Catholic minority to dethrone her, with the probable consequence of a religious war in England.

The Puritan experiments

It is certain that a no less dedicated body of Puritans and Protestant extremists would have risen against any Catholic seizure of power. From the early years of Elizabeth's reign this Puritan element, strongest in London and the south-eastern counties, had made itself heard in complaints against the lingering traces of catholicism in ecclesiastical ritual and outlook; and although Elizabeth could not afford to take measures against protestant extremism in the early years of her reign, the efforts of Puritans in parliament, within the established

Church and in the country at large to bring about radical reforms were to cause almost as much trouble as the Catholic recusants. In Puritan eyes, the reformation of the English church had stopped well short of its proper objective. By denying the authority of the Pope, substituting communion or 'the Lord's supper' for the mass, introducing an English liturgy and casting out what were considered superstitious and idolatrous images from the churches, a welcome start had been made; but the Puritans were impatient to obliterate all traces of Catholic ritual from the new religion. The reason for their impatience lay in their refusal to admit that the Church of Rome was a Christian institution. The Anglican reformers had no such quarrel with catholicism. They granted that it was substantially the true faith, but corrupted and overlaid by false practices which had accumulated during the Middle Ages; and their stated purpose was to recover the genuine form of Christian worship as it had existed in the fourth and fifth centuries. To the Puritan this was not enough. In his belief, the only true and pure form of Christianity lay still further off, in an epoch before the early Fathers of the Church had produced the comment-aries on holy writ which constituted the basis of Christian learning. The Puritans wanted no commentaries, and no scholarly interpretations of scripture. Assured of their ability to grasp God's purposes without any such learned exposition, they asked for nothing more than the English Bible which Coverdale had given them, and such elders as they would themselves freely elect. To persuade them that matters of religious doctrine and practice should be determined by the secular authority of the Queen would be as difficult as to make the Catholics accept the same point.

The first dispute between the Puritans and the establishment arose over the question of the vestments to be worn by the new clergy. To many parish priests the decision to retain a form of dress associated with Catholicism seemed a betrayal of Protestant principle, and the injunction which prescribed the wearing of vestments was angrily resisted. It was argued that the priest should be at liberty to choose how he dressed, that the clergy should be distinguished by their be-haviour and not by special clothing, and that congregations would be confused by seeing these marks of the old religion in a church which purported to have rejected Catholic doctrine and ritual. Their protests were ignored, for the Queen could not allow her prerogative of deter-mining the order of religious services to be successfully challenged. Frustrated on this point, the Puritans brought their indignation to bear upon other relics of catholicism which had been allowed to remain—kneeling during the Lord's supper, making the sign of the cross at baptism, using a ring in the marriage ceremony, and supple-menting the services with organ music.

To us such protests seem merely quaint and absurd; partly because the Elizabethan dramatists—whose theatres became the target of puri-tan indignation and abuse—succeeded in making such scruples of conscience seem ridiculous. The ludicrous remark given to Ananias in

Ben Jonson's play, *The Alchemist*, 'Bells are profane: a tune may be religious', suggests how easily the oddities of Puritan outlook could be exploited by the comic satirist. But Jonson is being less than fair to his victims when he presents them as monsters of hypocrisy and greed, who use religion as a mask for self-aggrandisement and fraud; and by making it seem that the Puritans constituted a race apart, an outlandish and eccentric enclave on the fringe of Elizabethan society. Like the Catholic recusants, by the end of the century the Puritans had proved the sincerity of their faith by their readiness to endure persecution and death for their beliefs. When in 1566 Matthew Parker, Elizabeth's first primate, published his *Book of Advertisements* or notices directing how church services were to be conducted, over a third of the clergy in the diocese of London refused to comply with his directions. Hitherto it had been possible for the extreme Protestants among them to avoid such elements of ritual as they found incompatible with a reformed Church, but this had led to such diversity of practice that the Queen had felt obliged to require 'an exact order and uniformity' in all religious ceremonies. Parker's directions could only offend the extremists who saw antichrist in every survival from the past, many of whom preferred to give up their livings rather than put his orders into practice. Others persisted in their puritanism despite the archbishop's decree, and Parker was forced to make a further show of authority; but not all the bishops whom he required to discipline their clergy were ready to support his measures, for several of them shared the puritan dislike of vestments and ritual.

Here again popular Elizabethan literature is likely to mislead us by suggesting that the Puritans were a lower middle-class sect, without learning or social distinction. In fact, the movement found adherents nót only among Elizabeth's bishops and clergy, but among nobles, courtiers and members of parliament; nor were the universities untouched by it. The man who emerged as the leader of puritan thought in this early phase, Thomas Cartwright, was professor of divinity at Cambridge and a scholar of great talent. From this eminent position within the Anglican establishment, Cartwright threw his weight against the new order by declaring his belief that Elizabeth's moderate protestantism was in total conflict with the principles of the primitive Christian Church. He found no authority in the New Testament for a hierarchy of bishops and archbishops, and contended that it should be swept away, to be replaced by elected ministers and elders who would be responsible for ecclesiastical discipline. His arguments were too formidable to be ignored, for they were firmly based on the scriptures, and too dangerous to be allowed free expression. After being deprived first of his professorial chair and then of his fellowship at Trinity College, in 1574 Cartwright was forced to leave the country to avoid arrest. But although he ceased to trouble the ecclesiastical authority with his presence, the ideas which he had planted would continue to impel puritan attacks upon the bishops, upon Anglican ritual, and upon the control of the Church by a secular power.

The Puritans in parliament made a number of attempts to bring about reforms in the Church by constitutional means. Parliamentary assent had been a necessary part of the religious settlement at the beginning of Elizabeth's reign; and as the puritan sympathies of parliament increased it seemed possible that the terms of the settlement might be emended. But this was to reckon without the Queen, who stood rigidly upon her prerogative and refused to allow religious matters to be discussed without her assent. When Walter Strickland introduced a bill for the reform of the prayer book in 1571, he was summoned before the privy council and forbidden to appear in parliament. A year later two bills 'touching rites and ceremonies' were impounded by the Queen before they could be discussed. In the decade following parliament showed much greater temerity by agreeing to consider the radical proposal that all existing legislation concerning the Church should be repealed, and a system of calvinist discipline put in its place. Again the Queen refused to permit any discussion of the bill, and when Peter Wentworth tried to open the subject of parliamentary privilege he was committed to the Tower. We should resist the temptation to see Wentworth and others as martyrs in the cause of free speech; for although they were prepared to risk their lives in challenging the prerogative which stifled them, a puritan state would no more have permitted free speech or religious dissent among those of other beliefs than had Mary. It was not puritan faith itself which Elizabeth was acting against, but the refusal of the Puritans to acknowledge the secular authority which she expressed through the Church. She might allow them to dissent, as she was willing that Catholics should subscribe to their private faith so long as they paid outward respect to her religious establishment; but she would not permit either Catholic or Puritan to bring her authority into question. Nor would she allow the Puritans in parliament to introduce measures designed to harass their particular enemies, the English Catholics. When in 1571 parliament passed a bill which would have compelled the recusants not merely to attend Anglican services but to take communion, Elizabeth vetoed it.

By the middle of Elizabeth's reign it had become clear that the Puritans could not be persuaded to accept either episcopal authority or crown control of religious affairs, and that they would continue to resist the royal prerogative. After Edmund Grindal, who succeeded Parker as archbishop in 1575, had himself challenged the Queen over the matter of puritan 'prophesyings', Elizabeth found herself obliged to move against this rebellious element within the church. These 'prophesyings' had been organized by the clergy, who met weekly or fortnightly in several south-eastern dioceses to study and discuss the scriptures. They also set up courts of discipline to improve public morals, a practice which respected the puritan ideal of bringing the life of the community under the rule of its elected presbyters or elders. Not without reason, Elizabeth suspected that these meetings might encourage the growth of Puritanism among the laity who were allowed to attend the 'prophesyings' as audience; and she ordered Grindal to suppress them forthwith. But her archbishop stood firm, refusing to carry out her command and remonstrating that the Queen's peremptory demand was no better than the 'antichristian voice of the Pope'. The tone of the phrase is revealing; and after the abrupt departure of Grindal from Canterbury Elizabeth seems to have taken care that no puritan sympathizer took his place. The man she appointed, John Whitgift, had already proved his loyalty to her Church by resisting the growth of puritanism at Cambridge, where he had been Cartwright's main adversary. In his arguments with Cartwright, Whitgift did not choose to meet his opponent on the thorny ground of how the early Christian church had been organized: the point at issue was not whether their assumptions were correct, but whether the present time and circumstances were right for such a sweeping reformation of the Church as the Puritans proposed; 'whether . . . it may stand with godly and Christian wisdom to attempt so great an alteration as this platform must needs bring in, with disobedience to the Queen and law and injunctions of the church, and offence to many consciences'.

Elizabeth was not disappointed in her new archbishop. In 1583 he acted decisively against the Puritans among his clergy, by framing six articles which all priests were to accept without qualification; requiring them to recognize the Queen's supremacy over the Church, the book of common prayer and the Thirty-Nine Articles. He appointed an ecclesiastical commission to ensure that his test was rigorously applied, with the consequence that over two hundred members of the clergy in East Anglia and Kent were suspended. Those whom the commissioners summoned to their court were asked to take an oath binding them to return true answers to a searching interrogation of their religious belief and allegiance: if they incriminated themselves by their answers they were fined or imprisoned without right of appeal, and if they refused to take the oath they were sent as suspects to the Court of Star Chamber to be punished. This practice aroused strong puritan protests, for it introduced a form of legal procedure contrary to principles of English law. The suspects were not examined in public, they were condemned by evidence they themselves were compelled to give, and they were declared guilty by their examiners, without reference to a jury. Such extreme measures could only be justified by Whitgift's determination to remove the puritan clergy from the church, for in many parishes the minister was so popular that his congregation would have refused to give evidence against him. In consequence of Whitgift's measures, and of the deaths of several puritan leaders in the early 'nineties, by the closing decade of her reign Elizabeth seemed to have mastered this second threat to the authority of her Church.

The Stuart Church

Thus when James came to the throne in 1603 he found the established Church in no immediate danger. Persecution of the Catholics had seriously reduced their numbers; for many—like Donne himself—had yielded either to practical expediency or loss of faith in the old religion, whose traditions were now part of an age outside the experience of most Englishmen. The Puritan movement was temporarily without any strong leader, and the new king was sufficiently confident of his royal authority to suppress any stirrings of dissent. This he showed very early in his reign, when a body of Puritan ministers presented their Millenary Petition, for which they claimed the support of a thousand of the clergy. Their petition amounted to a deferential request that certain ritual practices which the Puritans had always resisted—the use of a ring in the marriage ceremony, and the sign of the cross in baptism—should be dropped, and that other established customs should be left optional, such as the wearing of cap and surplice by the clergy. James went so far as to allow a conference to be called at Hampton Court in 1604, where he himself presided over a debate between the heads of the established Church and four Puritans; but the Puritans obtained no other satisfaction from this conference than the airing of their views. Their arguments left James completely unconvinced, and at the end of the conference he told the Puritan speakers that he would either force them to conform to established practice or drive them out of his kingdom. His own speech

Woodcut from The Bishop's Last Goodnight, *1642.*

Where Popery and Innovations doe begin,

Onely Canonicall prayers

no afternoon sermons

So we desire it.

Then no Bishops

Bishops.

Citizens.

If they had ruld still, where had we been ?

left no doubt that he intended to see that his subjects respected 'one doctrine and one discipline', and that he would resist any attempt to weaken the authority of established religion as an attack upon his own prerogatives as king. His frequently repeated phrase, 'No bishop, no king', summarized his belief that those who wished to bring about new reformations in the Church were also likely to undermine his position as divinely appointed sovereign.

As king of Scotland before his accession to the English throne, James had enjoyed a much less eminent and powerful position. During the reign of Elizabeth the Scots had given themselves the kind of presbyterian church that the English Puritans hoped for, which did not allow the king to impose his own policy upon ecclesiastical matters. James was naturally gratified by the supremacy in Church affairs which he acquired as king of England, and just as naturally disposed to react strongly against Puritan attempts to weaken the power of his bishops, who did most to uphold the doctrine of divine right which James adopted. For this reason he gave his full support to the bishops against their Puritan opponents in parliament, and they in return encouraged their flocks to offer no resistance to the king's decrees. Thus a situation was brought about in which neither Church nor State could be criticized; for criticism of the king was regarded as blasphemous, and opposition to the established religion treated as seditious. To impose such checks upon free discussion at a time when traditional assumptions about political and religous authority were being actively questioned could only increase resistance to the king and his bishops, though for the moment the opposition was not strong enough to challenge their reactionary power. When it came, the popular rebellion was more determined because its grievances had been suppressed for so long.

More than this, the combined authority of Church and Crown had deliberately outraged Puritan feeling by a number of ill-advised acts, some of which attracted popular sympathy to the Puritan cause. In 1624 it became illegal to print or to publish any book dealing with religion or church government without official approval—a form of censorship designed to protect the establishment against its Puritan opponents, who by this date were incensed by the king's assumption of divine right. The Arminians, the supporters of a high Anglican movement within the Church, were free to argue in favour of this divine prerogative as noisily as they wished, while all Puritan objections were to be silenced. When this edict against unlicensed printing was strengthened in 1637, a number of Puritan writers including William Prynne and John Lilburne suffered punishment by mutilation, whipping or the pillory for their pamphlets against the king's religious policy; but the great crowds who watched these scenes of cruelty, and who heard their victims' appeals for individual liberty, saw their savage treatment as evidence of tyranny. More popular indignation was aroused by attempts in 1618 and 1633 to crush the Puritan opposition to Sunday games and sports after church service,

Portrait of James I by Simon de Passe, 1616.

HENRICUS PACIFICI

Crounes haue their compasse, length of dayes their date,
Triumphes their tombes, felicitie bee fate :
Of more then earth, can earth make none partaker,
But knowledge makes the KING most like his maker.

Simon Passæus sculp: Lond.   Ioh: Bill excudit.

which were a traditional feature of English country life. With the growth of Puritan feeling, such recreations were coming to be regarded as ungodly, and in some parts of England Sunday games were actually suppressed by local authorities. The king replied to this move by ordering a declaration permitting lawful sports to be read from the pulpit throughout the kingdom. This edict was probably designed to discourage discussion of state affairs, to which men might turn if Sunday games were banned, rather than to preserve a venerable custom; but in the changing temper of the times this attempt to legitimize behaviour which a great number of the king's subjects considered sinful could only bring his divine right more deeply into question. He aroused further popular feeling by an order of 1622 which severely limited the range and subject matter of sermons to be preached by the clergy. Commentary upon texts taken from the creed or the Lord's prayer did not allow the preacher to pursue the line of argument which congregations had come to expect, and which for the Puritan was the most vital part of the service: the direct application of texts from Holy Writ to the political and ecclesiastical issues of the times. By this move the establishment silenced another source of criticism, and sharpened the desire for reform which it feared.

Such measures had the effect of widening the differences between Anglican conformity and puritanism. Under Elizabeth the Puritan objections to the established form and ritual of the English church were not severe enough to prevent his joining in its services. Many of the clergy were in general sympathy with Puritan aims and outlook, not disposed to challenge the crown's prerogative in ecclesiastical matters but sharing the Puritan dislike of customs and of ritual that they felt to be unreformed elements of catholicism. Such members of the clergy and their congregations would not have regarded themselves as Puritans, partly because the state still allowed a degree of latitude in religion which gave them a place within the established Church. Under James and Charles this degree of latitude was reduced to the point where those with Puritan inclinations and sympathies were forced outside the Anglican community. Typical of the measures which completely alienated an important part of the Anglican congregation was the directive of 1640 that the altar should be set at the east of the church and railed off, and that worshippers should bow towards the altar when they entered the church, and again when they left. To many this seemed a revival of popery, and an outraging of the Protestant ideal behind the Reformation; and by this date the king had identified himself so closely with the Arminianism of his bishops that those who wished for a radical reform of the Church knew themselves committed to a struggle against the sovereign. In this way the controversy over matters of religious outlook and practice merged with political issues which eventually could only be settled through civil war and the execution of Charles.

In its simplest terms, the war between king and parliament was the manifestation of a struggle between traditional loyalties and the demands of individual conscience, which gave men the will and determination to oppose the established power of sovereign and bishop. There was much blindness and bigotry on both sides. It is too great a simplification to suggest that where the royalists were the defenders of prerogative, their opponents were the guardians of liberty and justice. But it seems true to say that where the royalists were interested in preserving a traditional system of authority under the king, which did not allow the subject to criticize or obstruct his decisions, the parliamentarians were impelled by a genuine concern with the rights of the individual to challenge law and custom where they caused injustice or strained private conscience. In this respect they were breaking away from a constitutional system essentially unchanged since the late Middle Ages, and reshaping traditional ideas about the relationship between king and subject. In consequence, the authoritarian basis of English society was being weakened, and the individual was gaining a greater measure of personal freedom and protection under the law.

This did not come about at once. During the Commonwealth, Puritan control of English life piled so many restrictions and moral prohibitions upon the common man that, two years after Cromwell's death, the nation rose against this restrictive regime and welcomed back Charles II as king. The restoration of monarchy was a second manifestation of the people's new-found power. They would now be governed by their consent, and not by virtue of any unalienable right in the ruler himself. The break with the constitutional past was complete, and with its passing many ideas and attitudes which had maintained a tenuous link with the previous age disappeared for good. When Dryden, referring in 1670 to the work of Shakespeare and Jonson, calls it the poetry 'of the last age', he seems to be looking back over a vast expanse of time. In fact barely fifty years had passed; but in those years literature, like society itself, had undergone profound changes. Dryden was right to suggest the extent of the transformation. An exhausted tradition had succumbed to pressures aroused by its own inflexibility and resistance to change, and had been replaced by the vigorous and confident outlook of a new society, eager to demonstrate its independence of the past.

3   The intellectual background

Any discussion of Donne's intellectual background can be expected to begin by remarking that during his lifetime the frontiers of knowledge were being vigorously pressed back, and that the excitement of discovery was gradually qualified by the doubts which new facts and theories brought to bear upon the traditional structure of belief. The discussion may go further than this, and assert that by undermining the authority of the old science this influx of new ideas had a deeply disturbing effect upon religious and intellectual outlook; and that much of the evident pessimism and anxiety of Jacobean literature can be attributed to the crumbling of faith in an established order of things. Donne himself, in his *First Anniversary*, is often brought in as witness to the truth of this assumption. Whether we accept this view or not, it is clear that new ideas about universal order, the nature of man and the aims of scientific study which were produced in Donne's lifetime helped to form the body of new science which, by the end of the seventeenth century, had replaced traditional habits of thought and belief over a great range of subjects. We have some encouragement, therefore, to regard the age of Donne as a bridge joining an old and a new philosophy, or as a sometimes confused interval between waning of one intellectual authority and the enthronement of its successor; and to expect of Donne some direct commentary upon the struggle of ideas, or evidence in his poetry of the uncertainty which it caused. We shall be in a position to judge how far Donne was affected by the intellectual upheaval of his times, and to what extent his work reflects new philosophical interests, when we have some acquaintance with both traditions of thought.

Ancient opinion

The old philosophy, which retained its authority until the end of the sixteenth century at least, was a medieval compilation of ideas drawn from much earlier sources. The philosophers of the Middle Ages had no talent for original work in the various fields of scientific enquiry, and too much respect for the great speculative thinkers of the ancient world to question their teaching. Medieval learning in the fields of astronomy, physics, medicine, cosmography and biology, as in such less important subjects as dream lore and physiognomy, was firmly based on the received opinions of Aristotle, Pliny, Ptolemy, Galen and other ancient scientists whose works made up a comprehensive body of knowledge. The fact that these writers were pagans whose pre-Christian era denied them the full illumination of truth did not prevent the medieval Church—the immediate source of contemporary learning—from recognizing the importance of their work, or from accepting it as the embodiment of scientific truth about the nature of man and his universe. Some modifications had to be made where the ancient philosophers' opinions were at variance with Christian doctrine, but these were not great enough to change the essential form and character of the ideas which the Church absorbed. The main contribution of the medieval Schoolmen to this body of knowledge was to collate and arrange its beliefs into an organized scheme, relating its parts together and educing the patterns and correspondences which were to appeal so strongly to the Elizabethan mind. The writer John Maplet in 1581 adopts a familiar demonstration when he observes:

> Amongst all kinds of birds the eagle is president; among beasts the lion. In fresh and salt waters the mightiest fishes rule, as the whale in the sea and the pike in pools. Man ruleth over all living creatures; and in man, compounded of body, soul and understanding, the soul commandeth over the body, and the understanding over the desire.

He sees the correspondence extending to the family, whose head rules over its various members, and then to the state, where a sovereign or governor is set over the people as political ruler. The habit of thinking in such parallel terms, which Scholastic outlook directly encouraged, must be reckoned as an influence upon Elizabethan poetry when Shakespeare, 'heaping examples', builds up a list of like actions or qualities to reinforce an argument:

> As many arrows, loosed several ways,
> Come to one mark; as many ways meet in one town;
> As many fresh streams meet in one salt sea;
> As many lines close in the dial's centre;
> So may a thousand actions, once afoot,
> End in one purpose.
> Henry V, I. ii. 106–10.

Belief in the correspondences which related events throughout the hierarchies of created life was more than a picturesque fancy. By defining the sympathetic links between beings and substances of like nature, and showing the ordered design to which the myriad forms of universal life had been shaped, the old philosophy gave a close-knit unity to the whole of creation. Every being, however, trivial, had its appointed function in the cosmic scheme: every phenomenon and feature of the material world had its useful purpose; for the earth and the system of heavenly bodies surrounding it were the handiwork of the divine architect who made nothing at random or without its place in the great moving fabric of the universe. To discover the purpose which individual objects and creatures served within this unified design, and not to study their actual behaviour, was the aim of medieval science. It was not until the rise of experimental science in the seventeenth century that the erroneous beliefs of the old philosophy were brought to light. Assumptions which had gone unchecked for nearly two millenia were put to the test, and found to be mistaken. The new science could justifiably claim to be substituting exact knowledge for venerable hearsay; but the price of this more reliable information was the loss of the comforting assurance that the universe was centred on man, and that all its creatures—trees, minerals, birds, planets, insects, four-footed beasts—had specific places and functions in the minutely organized design which God had set upon his work.

The frame of order

The general form of this universal design will be familiar to readers of Elizabethan literature. It may be helpful to begin not by describing the Ptolemaic system of planets, moving about the fixed point of the earth, but with the simple proposition that, by God's special appointment, 'all things in the world serve to the community and use of mankind, whom God had made lord and master of all'. The opening chapter of Genesis left no doubt about the sovereignty imparted to man over all other forms of life. Man was not merely invited but bidden to regard the world as his own, created for his use and benefit; and to see all other creatures as existing to serve his purposes. The beasts produced flesh and skins so that he might be fed and clothed; trees had been created to supply him with timber for houses and boats; the earth contained metal so that he might possess tools and arms; the sun existed to give him warmth and light, and the stars to guide him through the darkness. The creation of man could be explained by seeing a need for God to be praised by a being capable of appreciating his goodness: the rest of creation then fell into God's design by ministering to man's needs.

Modern man has outgrown the habit of supposing that universal life revolves about him and exists for his exclusive benefit: we know ourselves to be the inhabitants of an unremarkable planet, held by the influence of a sun itself dwarfed by the magnitude and brilliance of distant stars, in a universe whose full extent we have no means of computing. What we know of the sheer immensity of cosmos, and of the insignificance of our own tiny planet, makes it impossible to believe that man is the centre of universal attention, and the being whom all other creatures exist to serve. But before Copernicus suggested that the earth did not stand at the centre of an easily imaginable universe, it was difficult to reach any other conclusion. The Hebraic view of man's dominating rôle was confirmed by Ptolemaic astronomy, which saw the sun and the other planets acting as satellites to the earth. Thus together Holy Writ and ancient science encouraged man to consider every other part of creation as determined by his needs and directly related to himself.

With this encouragement it is not surprising that the old philosophy should have taken man as its central principle, seeking to explain natural phenomena by showing their beneficial effects upon man's life, and the wisdom of the order which had disposed them to man's advantage. The sun, according to Ptolemy, was placed midway between the earth and the sphere of the fixed stars which limited the heavens; having the moon, Mercury and Venus on one side, and Mars, Jupiter and Saturn on the other. The arrangement was fitting; for the size and brilliance of the sun made it like a king among the planets, and his station gave him three attendants on either side. But there was a more practical reason why the sun should have been set midway between earth and the fixed stars: that in any other position the sun would have given either too much or too little heat to sustain life on earth. 'For if the sun were placed next to the earth,' John Maplet explains in another passage of his *Dial of Destiny*,

> the earth by his excessive heat must needs be brent up and consumed, and all things and creatures also upon the earth must needs die and perish; and contrariwise, if the sun had the highest place and were in that room where Saturn continueth, the earth here below should be void and destitute of sufficient heat, and all things living should periclitate and be in danger of decay.

It was proof of God's forethought and kindly concern for man that he had avoided these extremes, and given the sun a position that would most benefit life on earth. The placing of Saturn furthest from the earth was a similar mark of benevolence and wisdom; for this malignant planet, 'cold and dry, malicious and hurtful', had an entirely baleful influence upon living things; and it was as well for man that Saturn, 'of all other planets the cruellest, should be most remote and furthest off'. So long as medieval science concerned itself with explanations of this kind, taking the facts for granted and attempting to account for natural phenomena in terms of divine providence, it could learn nothing about the laws which govern the behaviour of material objects. On the other hand, it gave man the assurance of knowing that cosmos had been planned and fashioned according to his needs, and that every facet of its structure provided evidence of God's interest in the wellbeing of mankind.

Since the whole universe was God's personal handiwork, its beauty and symmetry were no more in question than the usefulness of its creatures. Seeing day matched by night, summer by winter and youth by age, the old philosophers supposed that such opposition was a fundamental principle of created life, and that every being and object had its antithesis, towards which it felt a natural antipathy. This sense of a symmetrical weighing of type against antitype throughout creation prompted a further belief that the sea contained marine versions of all the plants and animals found on land, and that the same kind of symmetry extended to geographical features of the southern hemisphere. Thus when Magellan discovered a south-west passage into the Pacific—mistaking Tierra del Fuego for the tip of an antarctic continent—the cosmographers supposed that a corresponding passage would be found in the north-west; for God's disposition of the four known land masses was as carefully contrived as the rest of his work.

Belief in the symmetry of creation found weighty support in the Aristotelian principle that all material objects were constituted of one or more of four elemental substances—earth, water, air and fire; and that in these elements the opposite qualities of hot and cold, wet and dry, were held in balance. The natural antipathy between fire and water—one hot and dry, the other cold and wet—gave each of these two elements a restraining influence over the other; and in the same way the heavy element of earth was offset by the lightness of air. The medieval mind saw each of the elements struggling to assert itself over the other three, with consequences that would be disastrous for life on earth. The form of such a universal cataclysm is suggested by Lear, when he calls upon the elements of air, water and fire to destroy all living creatures:

> Blow, winds, and crack your cheeks: rage, blow!
> You cataracts and hurricanoes, spout
> Till you have drenched our steeples, drowned the cocks!
> You sulphurous and thought-executing fires,
> Vaunt-couriers of oak-cleaving thunderbolts,
> Singe my white head!
>
> King Lear III. ii. 1–6.

But again the providence of God had placed safeguards upon the destructive potential of the elements, so that no such disaster could occur. The antipathy of water to fire, and of earth to air, assured that each element was kept in check by the contrary nature of its counterpart, and that no single element could gain ascendency over the others. From time to time—during great floods and tempests, or a summer of great heat—it might appear that the elemental balance had been disturbed; but always order reimposed itself through the resistance of a second element, and the disposition of the whole system towards stability.

Elements and humours

Since all things were compounded of the elements, man himself was framed of these four substances: he breathed air, was kept warm by the elemental fire in his bodily constitution, and took the liquid element of blood from water; and at death the heavier parts of his body reverted to earth, from which they were made. The element of fire was, in addition, responsible for the indispensable condition of man's bodily existence—the spirit of life itself; which as the Elizabethan psychologist Timothy Bright explained, had its origins in very thin blood, 'which being purified and as it were distilled with the hotness of the heart, engendereth a most subtle breath, much like a flame of fire; which passeth from the heart, and walking throughout the whole body, doth minister and yield unto every member a lively heat, which is called vital spirit'.

There was the same need to preserve an elemental balance within man's body as in the macrocosm, and for similar reasons. Undue preponderance of one element threw his constitution out of gear, and produced illness whose nature reflected this imbalance. To give a more accurate explanation of disease, and a clearer basis for medical treatment, the old philosophy held that the body contained four fluids called 'humours', each corresponding to one of the elements; and that good health depended upon their harmonious relationship. The element of fire gave its hot, dry quality to choler; a humour which in excess produced burning fevers. When Donne suggests, in *A Fever*, that his wife's illness might be the fire which 'shall burne this world', he is not being as fanciful as a modern reader might suppose. The watery element had a corresponding element in phlegm, whose preponderance could be recognized in dropsy and running colds; and the earthy humour of black bile was the cause of melancholy and depression. The remaining element, air, shared its warm moist quality with the humour of blood; and by imparting its characteristic lightness to the constitution, encouraged liveliness and gaiety to offset the depression arising from black bile. Excess of blood led to illnesses such as apoplexy, which might be relieved by bleeding the patient, to reduce the preponderance of this humour.

Ideally, the four humours should be so equally balanced that body and mind should remain in perfect health; but as from time to time the elements became unstabilized and produced floods and tempest, so the human constitution tended to favour one or other of the humours; and the temperament developed with a particular bias for some characteristically 'humorous' form of behaviour and outlook. In the sixteenth century as during the Middle Ages, individual temperament was referred to as 'complexion'; a term which now means only the facial colouring by which temperament could be recognized. Of the four complexions—sanguine, phlegmatic, choleric and melancholic—each had its characteristic marks in bodily appearance and manner. According to Galen, the sanguine man would be found to be 'of a purple and ruddy colour; soft, warm, and smooth-skinned; comely of stature and of reasonable feature; fleshly bodied and a little rough; auburn haired, red or yellow bearded, and comely bushed'— that is, with a great spreading head of hair.

Galen, and the generations of medical practitioners who followed his beliefs, saw blood as the best of the humours—'this lovely and amiable juice', as one Elizabethan writer described it—and supposed that the sanguine man would be distinguished by his good temper, robust physique, personal charm and liveliness. A preponderance of any of the other three humours was much less of an advantage. In the choleric man, natural moisture was severely reduced by the undue heat of 'the great store of choler which is in him'; and the resulting dryness impeded healthy growth and quickly exhausted the vitality of the body. Such men were found to be 'naturally fierce, arrogant, imperious, stately, untractable and unruly'; and could be recognized by their mean stature, leanness, rough skin and frizzled hair, as well as by their quickness of movement and rapid speech. Very different was the temperament of the phlegmatic man, whose cold, moist complexion made him naturally sluggish and drowsy; whose body was fat and pallid, and whose wits were feeble, being 'drowned in moist quality and cold humour' which left him stupefied and incapable. But least fortunate was the melancholic man; for where healthy life and growth required warmth and moisture, the mixture of dry and cold in his complexion threatened him with decay, and deprived him of all lively energy and good spirits. This disordered state of health might be brought about by prolonged grief or suffering; and could also be produced by exhausting the mind by studying too hard, 'by leading a peakish and solitary life, by hunger, penury, and strict fare; or else by using some kinds of nourishments whereby such men brought themselves into a cold and dry distemperature'. A man suffering from such a disorder would be ill-advised to eat root vegetables taken from the earth, for they would increase his imbalance towards melancholy; in the same way as eating fish from the cold, moist element would increase phlegm, and highly spiced food would increase choler.

Where modern medicine determines diet by calculating the amount of protein or vitamin which a given food contains, the old philosophy made its recommendations in the belief that every kind of meat and drink took on the properties of its natural evironment or source: that because birds lived in the air their flesh would contribute to the associated humour of blood, and that wine gave merriment and liveliness by adding to the vital spirits which animated the whole body. We may find such beliefs as absurd as the many scientific assumptions which the old philosophy promoted without ever examining the facts; but there is something humanly attractive in the notion that living creatures share the qualities and character of their environment, and are related by natural ties which the layman easily understands. Here again we see the strong basic tendency of the old philosophy to bring things into relationship and association: refusing to regard the universe as a random collection of objects and creatures—stones, planets, flowers, carnivores—dissociated by species, and existing in separate compartments. The whole universe was one entity, and through its network of sympathy and correspondence every single part was in communication with the rest.

Alchemy

The belief that all created objects were organized into systems and relationships supported one of the most persistent hopes of the old science—that of discovering the so-called philosophers' stone, by which base metals could be transmuted into gold. Like algebra, alchemy was one of the sciences brought to Europe during the Middle Ages by the Moorish invasion of Spain; but it proved to be a less useful form of knowledge. What persuaded generations of alchemists to waste time, money and ingenuity in a fruitless search for the philosophers' stone was a characteristic assumption that the metals, like all other created things, formed a hierarchy in which each kind had its appointed place. It followed from this that each metal was distinguished from the others not merely by its physical qualities but by its place in the natural order; so that to the medieval mind the sovereignty of gold or the baseness of lead were attributes as real as their weight and colour. The kingly quality of gold, the alchemists seem to have supposed, came in part from its inclusiveness: it summed up the qualities of metal as comprehensively as a king did those of his subjects, and in this way represented an epitome of their individual natures. If this were so, they evidently argued, it must be possible to make gold by combining elements of all the basic metals and related substances, like clay and ashes. This belief stands behind the numberless attempts of medieval alchemists to combine what they hoped were the right ingredients in the true proportions, so that when their mixture melted the result would be pure gold. The Canon's Yeoman asks his fellow-pilgrims in Chaucer's tale (lines 758–63):

> What sholde I tellen ech proporcion.
> And bisye me to telle you the names
> Of orpyment, brent bones, iren squames,   [scales.]
> That into poudre grounden been full smal;
> And in an erthen pot how put is al,
> And salt yput in, and also papeer,
> Biforn thise poudres that I speke of heer?

'Thise poudres' suggest the special ingredient which every alchemist trusted to bring the final transformation about; though for this much more was required than a simple melting of elements. Chaucer's Yeoman, who has been assistant to an alchemist, speaks of the work of 'sublymyng, amalgamyng and calcenyng,' and of the apparatus needed for this long process; the 'sondry vessels maad of erthe and glas,' urinals, descensories.

> Violes, crosletz, and sublymatories,
> Cucurbites and alambikes eek,
> And othere swiche, deere ynough a leek.

The lists of ingredients and apparatus are still longer in Jonson's play, *The Alchemist*, which was first performed in 1610. By this date alchemy had fallen into general disrepute by its long-standing association with such cheating and trickery as both Chaucer and Jonson describe; but so far as the scientific theory could be held apart from the frauds which it encouraged, there was still no reason to doubt its central assumption. Jonson's villains offer a different explanation of the scientific principle involved in the transmutation of metals. It would be absurd, Subtle argues, to suppose that gold suddenly came into existence in its perfect state: nature first creates a rough and imperfect substance, and then gradually refines it. The task of the alchemist is to accelerate this process by giving base metal the qualities which gold acquires through its long natural maturing, so that the change can occur overnight. To us, this idea must appear even more absurd than the other, but it conformed with the Elizabethan belief that gold was the final expression of qualities which the other metals shared to a smaller extent. Here again, the old philosophy insisted upon likeness and relationship within its hierarchies, and assumed that the character which philosophers attributed to an object were indeed part of its nature.

Maps of Wit

The sense of correspondence and relationship between objects entirely different in form and species directly encouraged the natural impulse of the poet to discover likenesses in things apparently dissimilar and unconnected. When Donne came of age, a vogue for witty writing gave further encouragement to the poet to seek out relationships that were sometimes absurdly improbable or fanciful; but such strained comparisons as Donne himself contrives may contain an element of seriousness. The old philosophy itself proposed connections between planets, animals and stones hardly less bizarre to modern judgment than the old associations which metaphysical poetry came to offer. The link between Scholastic beliefs and poetic practice was strengthened by the taste for intellectual attitudes and allusions in later Elizabethan writing, which developed with the widespread interest in formal rhetoric, described in a later chapter of this book. Wit, in its broad Elizabethan sense, could be displayed by references to ideas and beliefs of the old philosophy, which represented the only body of organized scientific opinion available to writers of the age. It is in this spirit that Shakespeare makes Maria compare Malvolio's face to 'the new map with the augmentation of the Indies'; an image both fantastic and learned, though referring to one of the discoveries which were proving the limitations of the old science.

The ancient geographers had assumed, reasonably enough, that the earth was divided into three continents meeting about the Mediterranean, which formed the physical centre of the known world. Their mistake was brought to light by the voyage of Columbus in 1492; and in the century following numerous expeditions and navigations to both the Americas revealed the magnitude of the error. In this

Map of the world showing Drake's circumnavigation of 1586–8,

VERA TOTIVS EXPEDITIONIS NAVTICÆ

DIEV ET MON DROIT

Porto Novæ Albionis

Portus Iavæ maioris

major respect at least the old science had been proved fallible, and we might expect to find a marked decline in the authority of its cosmographers in consequence, and a rejection of the intellectual habits which they had encouraged their readers to adopt. In fact neither happened. Instead, while sixteenth-century navigators, merchants and poets agreed in placing America firmly on the map, they continued to respect established authority by speaking as though the world had only three parts. This ambivalence of outlook is well illustrated by Donne himself, who in one poem can address his mistress as 'my America! my new-found-land', yet in another adopt the assumption of the old cosmography that three continents make up the world:

> On a round ball
> A workman that hath copies by, can lay
> An Europe, Afrique, and an Asia,
> And quickly make that which was nothing, all.
> *A Valediction: of Weeping*

Frobisher's attempts to find the North-West passage, the efforts to colonize Virginia, and Ralegh's expedition up the Orinoco were all too well publicized for the reality of this new continent to be doubted; yet Donne's conceit shows that even an unusually intelligent Elizabethan could continue to write as though the old cosmography had not been disproved. Although he knew that there were not three continents but four, the habit of thought implanted by traditional beliefs was evidently too deep-rooted to be checked, even when it was so obviously erroneous. Whatever the facts of the situation, which were fully acknowledged where practical considerations of trade and navigation were involved, in other respects Donne and his contemporaries seem to have found it more convenient to ignore the new map of the world, and to return to the appealing conception of a world divided into three neighbouring land-masses. This impulse to leave America out of account is not likely to have been motivated by respect for the old cosmography alone. It seems more probable that the habit of expecting all creation to be laid out according to a logical design made it difficult to accept the existence of America imaginatively. However vast, it stood entirely outside the ordered scheme of the old world, refusing to combine with the other three continents in the intelligible order which must inform all the work of God. America might be accepted as a geographical fact, but its existence seems to have posed theological questions which Donne's age was not ready to examine.

Before the bases of empiricism had been established, there was no immediate case for discarding a scientific theory when it had been shown to conflict with observable fact. Such evidence did not form the basis of Scholastic science, which had been laid down dogmatically or by arguing the likely behaviour of objects from their supposed natures. Thus it was believed that, because it was heavier, a large stone fell more rapidly than a small one; where a practical test would have shown that they fell at the same rate. But where intellectual outlook was dominated by the authority of Scholastic dogma, there could be no inclination to submit beliefs to any form of practical test; for this was not the means by which the philospher arrived at the truth. The opinions held by Aristotle or Ptolemy were not to be regarded as hypotheses which later scientists might challenge and modify, but as statements of absolute fact to be pondered and repeated. Bacon was to complain justly that 'knowledge derived from Aristotle and exempted from liberty of examination, will not rise again higher than the knowledge of Aristotle,'* but the habit of testing theories experimentally, and of searching for truth in the actual behaviour of natural objects, rather than in received opinions, had still to establish itself. During Donne's lifetime, intellectual curiosity reached a point where a few outstanding scientists began to make such observations, and to question some of the fundamental assumptions of the old philosophy; but as yet there was no general movement towards the rejection of its authority. Some of the new ideas aroused hostility and contempt, but for the most part they seem to have been met with indifference and incomprehension. It is not difficult to understand why. The old philosophy was a closely integrated system of belief, which could not be dismembered piecemeal. Once fallibility was admitted, the whole system was in danger of falling apart; for such a concession would involve admitting not only that it was mistaken on some particular point, but that its character- istic method of arriving at the truth by what Bacon called 'tumbling up and down in their own reason and conceits' was completely un- reliable. To recognize that scientific truth must come through pain- staking observation of nature, as Bacon insisted, required a major readjustment of intellectual outlook, which could not be accom- plished overnight. Further, before the old philosophy could be abandoned, an alternative system of belief had to stand ready to take its place. In Donne's lifetime, only a few tentative steps had been taken towards the position which was securely established with the publication of Newton's *Principia Mathematica* in 1687. Even when faults in the old system were admitted, there could be no will to exchange the current conception of universal law for a still unformu- lated body of new ideas. Over a long transitional period, new scientific discoveries had to be accommodated, with varying degrees of dis- comfort, within the system of belief which they contradicted.

One of the earliest and most persistent of them was the argument that the earth did not, after all, stand at the centre of cosmos, but was a satellite of the sun. This argument had been advanced by Pytha- goras six centuries before Christ, but to have regarded the earth as a moving observatory would have greatly complicated primitive astro- nomy, and—no less serious—the theory did not conform with the religious doctrine of the medieval world. Pythagorean astronomy was therefore forgotten, and when Copernicus revived its argument

Advancement of Learning I. iv.

in 1543 he appeared to be making a new and startling suggestion. The Church of Rome moved to defend orthodox faith by placing *De revolutionibus orbium coelestium* on its index of proscribed books, but although—as this action admitted—Copernicus was threatening to unsettle the basis of established belief, his theory seems to have made little impression upon the general outlook of the age. Some modern commentators have too readily assumed that an assault upon so central a tenet of scientific thought could only have produced disorder and uncertainty. If it did, the disturbance was either very localized or well concealed. More probably, Copernicus simply failed to shake popular faith in a Ptolemic axiom whose truth was self-evident to the humblest observer: that the earth stood still in the heavens, while the sun revolved about it. Even in this more enlightened age we speak of sunrise, not of earthdip; for intellectual judgment has little force against man's instinctive sense of standing on a motionless earth. The threat posed by Copernicus was largely academic: an affront to theological opinion but not an idea that could distress the common man, whose observation told him how foolish it was. Those English writers of the early seventeenth century who resist the Copernican theory refer to him in amusement and contempt, not with anger or with the sense of resisting a dangerous heresy. Donne, we shall see later, was among those who disbelieved Copernicus but treated his ideas indulgently.

Most English readers must have become acquainted with Copernicus through Thomas Digges, whose *Perfit Description of the Coelestiall Orbes* was published in 1576. His simple presentation of the argument makes it easier to understand why this challenge to the old philosophy was so quietly assimilated. If the authority of Ptolemy is brought into question, there is no hint of disrespect for the power which ordains universal order, and no suggestion that God's wisdom is less admirable in this new cosmic design than in the old. To the contrary, Digges calls attention to the majesty and wondrousness of the great system by which the earth is contained:

> Herein can we never sufficiently admire this wonderful and incomprehensible huge frame of God's work proponed [set forth] to our senses; seeing first this ball of the Earth wherein we move to the common sort seemeth great, and that in respect of the Moon's orb is very small; but compared with *orbis magnus* wherein it is carried, it scarcely retaineth any sensible proportion, so marvellously is that orb of annual motion greater than this little dark star wherein we live. But that *orbis magnus* being—as is before declared—but as a point in respect of the immensity of the immoveable heaven, we may easily consider what little portion of God's frame our elementary corruptible world is; but never sufficiently be able to admire the immensity of the rest: especially of that fixed orb garnished with lights innumerable, and reaching up in spherical altitude without end.

This passage serves as a helpful corrective to the assumption that the Copernican theory could only have aroused alarm and deep misgivings among Elizabethan readers. Copernicus continued to regard the sphere of the fixed stars as the motionless abode of angelic spirits, and its height above the earth as the measure of its spiritual purity; and his theory confirmed anew the inherent orderliness and beauty of the whole cosmic design. His argument introduced a new concept which disputed Aristotle's authority in one area of science, but except in the field of theology presented no radical challenge to the old tradition of thought. The notion that man did not, after all, stand at the centre of God's creation could be accepted without abandoning the Scholastic position to which it belonged. Alternatively the issue might be set aside with the kind of mild rebuke which Milton was to express through Raphael:

> Whether heaven move or earth
> Imports not, if thou reckon right; the rest
> From man and angel the great Architect
> Did wisely to conceal, and not divulge
> His secrets to be scanned by them who ought
> Rather admire.
>
> *Paradise Lost* viii. 70–5

The disturbing effect of the Copernican theory has been exaggerated by commentators of our own times who recognize its deeper implications. If Copernicus was right, then the whole system of Ptolemaic astronomy was based upon an error great enough to invalidate its picture of universal order, and it would be necessary to reject this traditional belief altogether. But to Donne and his contemporaries such a total rejection of Ptolemy would have been impossible. We do not discard one form of belief until an alternative offers itself, and until Newton published his *Principia Mathematica* much later in the seventeenth century no such alternative existed. A modern reader looking back over the centuries of new science sees Copernicus in a context which Elizabethans could not dream of. To us he is a bold forerunner of the scientific thought which was to develop a century later: to them he was hardly more than an amusing crank.

The impact of Galileo's discoveries upon the popular mind has probably been overstressed in much the same way. By observing the planets through the newly invented telescope, Galileo found that Jupiter had a number of attendant moons which moved about the greater body of the planet. This observation was in conflict with an important point of Scholastic doctrine, which asserted that the forces of change and decay did not extend beyond the sphere of the terrestrial moon. Above that—higher, to the Scholastic way of thinking, and thus in a purer form of existence—the planets were fixed in an unchanging, incorruptible order, wheeling about the earth with a regularity unmatched by any sublunary body. This sense of faultless perfection was seriously compromised by Galileo's discovery. Evidently the heavens

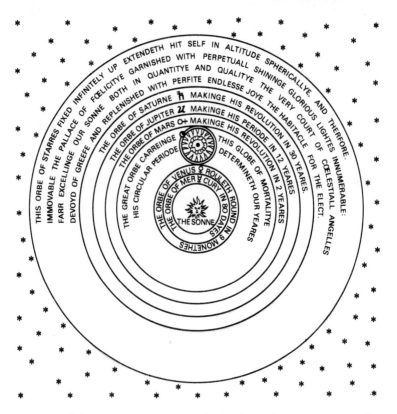

Diagram of the Copernican system, redrawn from Thomas Digges's Perfect description of the Celestial Orbs, *1576.*

contained satellites which recognized not the earth but Jupiter as their centre, and which did not conform to the great general principle which made all the planets turn about the same fixed point. Furthermore, above the sublunary sphere which was accepted as the boundary of change and decay were other moons, if Galileo's testimony could be believed; and a moon could only be associated with the forces of growth and decay which were held to extend no further than the sphere of mutability which enclosed the earth.

This was not the only blow which Galileo struck at the old philosophy, for from other observations he learned of the existence of sunspots. Such blemishes might be accepted in the moon, which lay within the sphere of change and decay; but physical blots could only be seen as evidence of imperfection which no philosopher of the old school could admit in the planetary system. When the professor of astronomy at Padua refused to look through Galileo's telescope to confirm his discoveries, he was not trying to obstruct the course of science. A scientist had not established the truth when he had proved a fact experimentally: he was not expected to establish truth at all, for that had been done centuries earlier by the Schoolmen. If facts and appearances sometimes conflicted with Scholastic doctrine, there could be no possibility of preferring a chance event to a settled opinion confirmed by ages of agreement. It is difficult for us to project ourselves intellectually into the Scholastic habit of working from written authority and of ignoring the actual behaviour of the natural world; but medieval science was firmly based upon such received opinion. There was no need to look through Galileo's telescope: the nature of the heavens had been defined by the greatest of philosophers, and a child's toy was not to disprove the teaching which had gone unchallenged for so many centuries. None the less, it was with the telescope that Galileo found the Galaxy or Milky Way to be composed of myriads of stars: a discovery to which Donne probably makes one of the earliest allusions in the first stanza of his poem *The Primrose*.

Profit, observation and experiment

This uncritical veneration for the voice of the long past was a feature of the old science which came under attack in Bacon's *Advancement of Learning*, published in 1605. As a long reasoned evaluation of the intellectual outlook of his times, the first book of the *Advancement* is probably both a more significant and a more potentially influential contribution to seventeenth-century thought than any of the scientific theories or discoveries that might be mentioned. This is not to say that Bacon's ideas had an immediate impact on seventeenth-century readers. The considerable interval of twenty-five years elapsed before the *Advancement* was published for the second time, and Bacon's importance as the forerunner of a new attitude to scientific learning was not fully appreciated until still later in the century. Few of his first readers can have been much affected by his arguments; but as his ideas lay germinating they helped to turn the movement of contemporary thought in a new direction, and to encourage a more radical questioning of traditional attitudes of mind. The simple, perceptive remark which he directs against the authority of the greatest of the old philosophers may have seemed merely rebellious: 'Knowledge derived from Aristotle and exempted from liberty of examination will not rise again higher than the knowledge of Aristotle'. [I. iv. 12]. But the remark forms part of an argument whose purpose is to encourage enquiry, and not simply to dethrone Aristotle. Pupils owe their teachers, Bacon declares, 'only a temporary belief and a suspension of their own judgement till they be fully instructed, and not an absolute resignation or perpetual captivity' [*ibid.*], and although it is right to give ancient authors their due, that respect must not prevent the general advance of enquiry, whose end is 'further and further to discover truth'. When he considers the defects and weaknesses of the prevailing attitudes towards knowledge, Bacon calmly challenges some of the central tenets which, in his clear-sighted view, have been responsible for stagnation and error in the field of scientific knowledge. Among the more important of them, he suggests, has been 'a kind of adoration of the mind and understanding of man', which has prompted philosophers to account for natural phenomena by working out a likely explanation in terms of divine purposes. The old scientists were confident of their ability to understand natural events by reasoning their causes, and did not trouble to make the observations which might have revealed the working of natural laws. 'Men have withdrawn themselves too much from the contemplation of nature,' Bacon complains, 'and have tumbled up and down in their own reason and conceits. . . . They disdain to spell, and so by degrees to read in the volume of God's works; and contrariwise by continual meditation and agitation of wit do urge and as it were invocate their own spirits to divine and give oracles unto them, whereby they are deservedly deluded' [I. v. 6]. This criticism is more serious than its measured tone may suggest, for it amounts to a thorough discrediting of the mode of scientific enquiry adopted by the old philosophers. Galileo's findings could be disregarded because their method was untraditional and invalid: truth lay in Holy Writ or the writings of the ancient astronomers, not at the further end of a telescope.

By joining issue with the Schoolmen on this crucial point, Bacon was shaking the fabric of their philosophy; but in discussing the greatest error of contemporary learning—'the mistaking or misplacing of the last or furthest end of knowledge'—he delivered a still greater blow against Scholastic tradition. The philosophers of the ancient world had studied their environment out of a desire for knowledge as disinterested as ever prompted scientific enquiry. The medieval Church inherited their findings without either their spirit of enquiry or their respect for scientific knowledge as an end sufficient in itself. Man was now to study the natural world in order to grasp the inexpressible wonder of divine creation, and thus to subordinate scientific enquiry to religious feeling. This attitude is expressed by Sir Thomas Browne in *Religio Medici*, published in 1642, when he remarks that 'Those highly magnify [God] whose judicious enquiry into his acts, and deliberate research of his creatures, return the duty of a devout and learned admiration'. The characteristic form of medieval enquiry which appealed so strongly to this well-trained physician is indicated in his comment:

In the causes, nature and affections [influences] of the eclipse of the sun and moon there is a most excellent speculation; but to propound farther, and to contemplate a reason why his providence hath so disposed and ordered their motions in that vast circle as to conjoin and obscure each other, is a sweeter piece of reason and a diviner point of philosophy.

Browne's 'why' could not be answered by an account of the natural forces and movements that are involved in an eclipse: his 'most excellent speculation' would end in an explanation of God's purposes in causing an eclipse to occur. The example shows how natural philosophy had become a minor province of theology, treated as an invitation to ruminate over the finally insoluble question of divine will and not to weigh, measure and observe the behaviour of natural objects. Bacon had already condemned such speculation by remarking that if human intellect cuts itself off from 'the contemplation of the creatures of God', and works upon itself 'as the spider worketh his web, then it is endless, and brings forth indeed cobwebs of learning, admirable for the fineness of thread and work, but of no substance or profit' (I. iv. 5).

The keyword of this argument is 'profit'. Bacon wished learning to be useful, as it could never be while it remained the form of agreeable diversion which Browne found it. Learning would attain its proper end, in Bacon's view, when this merely speculative element of thought had been separated from all that was purposeful and of practical interest in natural philosophy, 'that knowledge may not be as a courtesan, for pleasure and vanity only, or as a bondwoman, to acquire and gain to her master's use, but as a spouse, for generation, fruit and comfort' (I. v. 11). Although Bacon is understandably careful not to offend religious feeling, it is clear from his argument that the idea of studying natural phenomena in order to admire the ingenuity of God's handiwork was to him an irrelevant pursuit. Knowledge was to serve an essentially practical end; not by enriching its possessor but by enabling man to achieve what the arrogant modern phrase calls the control of his environment. In his picture of an ideal state where learning has been directed to such practical ends, Bacon describes a society organized about an institution for scientific research, whose head outlines their purposes as 'the knowledge of causes and secret motions of things; and the enlarging of the bounds of human empire, to the effecting of all things possible'.

New Atlantis was written later in Bacon's life, and published in 1627 a year after his death. Its ideas, and its prophetic glimpse into a future when telephones, submarines and refrigerators would have been invented, consolidate the position which Bacon takes up in *The Advancement of Learning* and build upon its suggestions. In his wish to have knowledge of the 'causes and secret motions of things' Bacon seems to be associating himself with the impulse that led Dr Faustus to destruction; but the fear of enquiring too far, which seems to be justified in Marlowe's play, was now beginning to lose its power of daunting research. The secret motions which Bacon's scientists set themselves to discover were not to be considered as forbidden to man's knowledge. In declaring their freedom to pursue enquiry beyond the bounds of theological approval—more simply, in divorcing natural philosophy from divinity—they were reducing the authority of God as it had been accepted hitherto. Whether for good or evil, desire for scientific knowledge was becoming more powerful than such traditional respect. This change of outlook reflected a

A seventeenth century compass.

slow but comprehensive shift in man's conception of his own nature and competence which eventually led him to abandon the old tradition of thought.

The scientific discoveries of the new age deserve to be remembered as milestones in the establishing of truth based upon observation and experiment. But as poets, Donne and his contemporaries were not directly involved in these discoveries; and a literary historian must be more concerned with the intellectual outlook which prompted Bacon to write his *Advancement*, or Harvey to make the enquiries that led him to discover the circulation of the blood. Such challenges and such discoveries came about as the result of a disposition to question and re-examine which was beginning to show itself after centuries of intellectual conformity; and this intellectual stirring may not have been confined to scientists. Something new was in the air which the sensitive antennae of a poet might have picked up and incorporated into his writing, not in explicit terms but as an echo of the changed attitude underlying the shift of scientific outlook. It is generally assumed that Donne's poetry gives body to these intellectual undercurrents, and that he expresses a direct interest in the outlook of the new science which his age was bringing into being. This suggestion is immediately attractive. It seems to explain why so many of Donne's images are taken from broadly scientific subjects, and why he adopts an argumentative method in developing his theme, where other Elizabethan poets seem to be impelled only by feeling. Despite its plausibility, however, this is a suggestion to be treated with reserve.

The fact is that Donne's scientific allusions are drawn entirely from the old philosophy. No alternative was open to him, for at the period of his *Songs and Sonets* at least, if not throughout his life, there existed no coherent body of thought which might have been recognized as a new scientific outlook. This fact has been obscured by the mistaken belief that in *The First Anniversary* Donne refers explicitly to 'the new philosophy': a mistake encouraged by Grierson's oversight in the introduction to his *Metaphysical Poetry*, where the line is misquoted. What Donne wrote was 'And new philosophy calls all in doubt,' and although a modern reader may reasonably suppose the phrase to carry much the same meaning, Donne is using 'philosophy' to mean the study of nature. He seems to be referring generally to the new ideas of his age, but in fact he intends a particular and limited reference to the Copernican theory, already half a century old. Donne uses the phrase again in *Sermon LXXX* when, discussing the impermanence of earthly things, he remarks: 'I need not call in new philosophy, that denies a settledness, an acquiescence in the very body of the earth, but makes the earth to move in that place where we thought the sun had moved: I need not that help, that the earth itself is in motion, to prove this.' The phrase appears again in his *Devotions*, a series of prose pieces recording the progress of a serious illness which Donne underwent in 1623. When the fever abates, and he is allowed to leave his bed, he writes:

I am up, and I seem to stand, and I go round; and I am a new argument of the new philosophy that the earth moves round. Why may I not believe that the whole earth moves in a round motion, though that seem to me to stand, when as I seem to stand to my company, and yet am carried in a giddy and circular motion as I stand?

(*Meditation XXI*)

With these examples before us, we have to abandon any notion that

Donne's 'new philosophy' involved a prevision of Newtonian physics, or the recognition of any other organized body of new scientific ideas. We have also to take the no less important point that Donne is so far from expressing anxiety over the Copernican theory that he can make it the subject of a light-hearted conceit. The passage describing himself as 'a new argument of the new philosophy' should send us back to *The First Anniversary* with a more critical awareness of Donne's tone. When he complains that, in consequence of the Copernican argument, 'The element of fire is quite put out' (l. 206) Donne is playing on two senses of the expression 'put out', and showing more witty detachment than disquiet. To judge from his playful remarks in the *Devotions*, Donne gave Copernicus very little serious consideration. Harvey, who published his discovery of the circulation of the blood well within Donne's lifetime, seems not to have persuaded Donne to revise his traditional belief that the heart served merely to heat the blood. In a sermon preached in 1626 Donne summed up his intellectual allegiance by remarking, in respect of man's knowledge: 'We look upon Nature but with Aristotle's spectacles, and upon the body of man but with Galen's, and upon the frame of the world but with Ptolemy's spectacles.' There can have been few members of his congregation for whom this generalization was not true, as it certainly was for the preacher himself.

The poet's position

We do not read Donne in order to learn about the old philosophy, nor did he write in order to air his knowledge. There are in fact fewer scientific allusions in his poetry than are sometimes supposed. The popular notion that his writing abounds in references to navigation, alchemy, mathematics, the elements and human anatomy needs only to be tested against a few poems to be seen as mistaken. Here and there we find the scientific analogies and parallels which were to become characteristic of metaphysical poetry: in *The Funeral* (ll. 9–11), for instance, where Donne follows the old anatomy in regarding the sinews as though they were nerves, feeding information to the brain:

> For if the sinewy thread my brain lets fall
>> Through every part,
> Can tie those parts, and make me one of all:

or in *The Dissolution* which speaks of the lover's

>> fire of passion, sighs of air,
> Water of tears, and earthly sad despair,

and affirms conventionally that these elements 'my materials be'. Another of the *Songs and Sonets* contains a well-known reference to the belief, shared by theologians and physicians, that the vital spirits served to unite the bodily and the spiritual identities of man (*The Ecstasy*, 61–4).

> As our blood labours to beget
> Spirits as like souls as it can,
> Because such fingers need to knit
> That subtle knot which makes us man.

But Donne's allusions to contemporary philosophy are seldom as elaborate or as specific as these passages suggest. Moreover, by isolating such references we may overlook their function in the poem, which is to support an argument and not to display Donne's learning. *The Funeral* continues, after suggesting its physiological parallel,

> These hairs which upward grew, and strength and art
> Have from a better brain,
> Can better do't:

maintaining that the bracelet of woman's hair which Donne wears can tie him together more effectively than the 'sinewy threads' in his own body. Similarly, in *The Ecstasy*, Donne uses the reference to the 'subtle knot' of man's mixed nature to argue that lovers' souls must not ignore their physical senses, but find expression through them. The illustration drawn from science or theology is not itself the focus of Donne's interest, but a means of bringing attention to bear upon the idea which he is working out. This is the aspect of his poetry which has probably caused most surprise, and in some ages given most offence, to Donne's readers; who suppose for the most part that poetry is concerned with passions and sensations rather than with dialectic, and that its images are drawn from the natural world rather than from the sciences. But Donne, as will be suggested in a later chapter, seems to have been imaginatively impelled to define his experience; and to serve this purpose his images had to have an exactness of meaning that sensation cannot render. His comparison of the separated lovers to 'stiff twin compasses'—or as we should say, to a pair of dividers—in *A Valediction forbidding Mourning* makes its point by excluding all terms of feeling, and by forcing us to consider the lovers' relationship in its starkly essential form. The oddity of the image, and its unlikeliness as a figure of love poetry, are incidental to Donne's purpose: what matters is the clarity and firmness of his definition, which only an intellectual parallel can provide.

Compasses, maps, globes and spheres suggest a common interest in navigation and cosmography, and encourage a modern reader to suppose that Donne took a lively interest in the geographical discoveries of his age. We should not press this point too far, but recognize that Donne also shows himself aware of the less momentous common affairs of his day. Thus he refers to the portraitist Hilliard, to the chronicler Holinshed, and to Bajazeth, a character in Marlowe's *Tamburlaine*. If at one time he speaks of America, at another he mentions Westminster, Aldgate and Charing Cross, and alludes to books which were the fashionable reading of the times. Such passages help to correct any impression that Donne's intellectual interests were limited to academic and scholarly subjects. They were far more comprehensive. It is the generality of his interests, both erudite and everyday, finding expression first through images of alembics and atomies, and then by referring to sundials and bedstaves, which should prevent us from assuming that Donne was either medieval or modern in outlook. He belonged to his time, and embraced its characteristic beliefs; more consciously than most of his contemporaries, perhaps, but not separated from them by any appreciation of how short a time the authority of the old philosophy had still to run. As a young poet, writing verse that was often challengingly bold and original, he might have been seen as the forerunner of a literary movement supported by a vigorous disposition to challenge and remould traditional ideas. As dean of St Paul's he had lost this defiant energy. The sermons reveal a sombre awareness of moral corruption, feeding itself on a pessimistic evaluation of man which lames the hope of an intellectual advance. 'We are all conceived in close prison,' he told his congregation in 1619, 'in our mothers' wombs we are close prisoners all; when we are born we are born but to the liberty of the house, prisoners still, though within larger walls; and then all our life is but a going out to the place of execution, to death.'

Donne's obsession with decay and mortality, embodied in the effigy in St Paul's Cathedral, was shared by other Jacobean writers who could not shake off the sense of moral contamination which man had inherited from the Fall. Their attitude of mind, and the defeatism it encouraged, were seen as a direct challenge to the new ideas which were slowly establishing themselves, and to the half-formed promise of progress in learning offered by Bacon. It became an urgent task of the new movement of thought to resist the pessimistic conviction of man's ignorance and helplessness which Donne's sermons admit so frequently. We should see the gloom and foreboding that darkens Jacobean outlook, perhaps, as the characteristic response of men whose familiar landmarks were crumbling, and who could not re-establish themselves in the world of mixed values and uncertain standards from which, after an interval of open confusion, the outlines of a new system would emerge. Donne was not among the handful who sensed in advance what this form was to be. Intellectually and by emotional inclination he was rooted in his epoch; coming of age during its great upsurge of optimism and self-confidence, and dying when the afterglow of Elizabethan splendour was about to be finally extinguished. His mind had been a storehouse crammed with current ideas and intellectual concepts drawn from sources which epitomized the nature and range of Elizabethan belief. It is significant that what his poetic followers borrowed from him most eagerly was the oddity or quaintness which Donne's intellectual figures had then acquired.

Monument at Chesterfield, Derbyshire, c. 1585.

4 The literary background

Metaphysical style

Donne is commonly considered as the great literary innovator of his age: a poet who although much less accomplished than Shakespeare, shaped for himself a much more individual style. Shakespeare emerged from the main stream of Elizabethan poetic tradition where Donne, it might seem, forced himself into the literary limelight by the sheer energy, impudence and originality of his writing. This view of Donne is put forcefully by Carew in his elegy to the dead poet, when he comments in a famous passage (lines 25–8):

> The Muses' garden, with pedantic weeds
> O'erspread, was purged by thee; the lazy seeds
> Of servile imitation thrown away,
> And fresh invention planted.

Set beside the flamboyance and lavishness of much Elizabethan verse—qualities which obviously appealed to Spenser, Marlowe and the young Shakespeare—the bare, taut, unceremonious language of the *Songs and Sonets* can make Donne seem like the poet of a different age and a distinct tradition. It would be unjust to deny the importance of the qualities which separate Donne from other Elizabethan poets and establish his individual greatness; but it would also be mistaken to suppose that Donne's 'fresh invention' was entirely independent of current trends of Elizabethan writing. Although much that Donne wrote was surprising, it was not always new; and in one major respect at least he was continuing to develop a line of interest which several Elizabethan poets had already found absorbing.

It was as monarch of wit that Carew finally described Donne, whose style in prose and poetry is dominated by a taste for intellectual argument and demonstration, often by means of the conceit: a fanciful or ingenious notion worked into the train of thought. Donne surpassed other poets by going further, by straining comparisons and relationships of idea to the point where they seem about to crack; but this extremism does not disguise Donne's association with a literary fashion which had been growing for at least twenty years before he began to write. The line of wit has its roots in formal rhetoric, which was being rediscovered and popularized during Shakespeare's boyhood. Its practices, schematized in such handbooks as Wilson's *Art of Rhetoric*, 1553, were taken up enthusiastically by writers of fiction and raised to a point of elaborate artifice in Lyly's *Euphues*, published in 1578. The subtitle of Lyly's prose tale, 'The Anatomy of Wit', defines his purpose. His story is a flimsy outline serving as basis for an astonishingly versatile display of rhetorical tropes and figures, arranged in counter-balancing patterns whose sense is always subordinate to Lyly's euphuistic style. The wit of his subtitle is displayed in the sheer inventiveness of his writing, which draws upon every variety of rhetorical figure to produce its fantastic embroidery of speech:

Alas Euphues, by how much the more I love the high climbing of thy capacity, by so much the more I fear thy fall. The fine crystal is sooner crazed than the hard marble, the greenest beech burneth faster than the dryest oak, the fairest silk is soonest soiled, and the sweetest wine turneth to the sharpest vinegar; the pestilence doth most rifest infect the clearest complexion, and the caterpillar cleaveth unto the ripest fruit; the most delicate wit is allured with small enticement unto vice, and most subject to yield unto vanity. If therefore thou do but harken to the Sirens thou wilt be enamoured: if thou do haunt their places and houses thou shalt be enchanted.

The attraction of this metronomic style soon palls, and after a blaze of popularity euphuism was to fall out of fashion as suddenly as it had burst upon Elizabethan readers; but the urge to display unwearied inventiveness that is so marked in Lyly's writing did not share his eclipse. The young Shakespeare's fondness for multiplying examples—one of the figures of formal rhetoric—is clearly shown by this characteristic passage of his first published work, *Venus and Adonis* (ll. 163–8).

Torches are made to light, jewels to wear,
Dainties to taste, fresh beauty for the use,
Herbs for the smell, and sappy plants to bear:
Things growing to themselves are growth's abuse.
  Seeds spring from seeds, and beauty breedeth beauty:
  Thou wast begot; to get it is thy duty.

The poet displays his wit by calling up a rapid series of illustrations to support the speaker's argument; but there is wit of a tougher kind in the argument itself. Where Lyly chooses images for an effect of colour and variety without disciplining his ideas at all strictly—sweet wine does not in fact produce the tartest vinegar—Shakespeare keeps a firm grip on the point being debated, and makes the illustrations serve this purpose. In this way his variation on Lyly's style acquires a much stronger intellectual element than euphuism had included, and Shakespeare gives impulse to a more demanding form of wit which depends more upon subtle presentation of ideas than upon sheer copiousness. He sometimes pursues this intellectual element of his poetry to the verge of mere cleverness (*Venus and Adonis*, 961–6):

93

O how her eyes and tears did lend and borrow;
Her eye seen in the tears, tears in her eye;
Both crystals where they viewed each other's sorrow:
Sorrow that friendly sighs still sought to dry.
    But like a stormy day, now wind, now rain,
    Sighs dry her cheeks, tears make them wet again.

We recognize here incipient forms of the conceit which Donne was to
make a conspicuous feature of his poetry. Shakespeare's play of
ideas aims at a pretty, half-comic effect, and stops where Donne would
begin to apply analytical pressure; but in this stanza Donne might
have found the starting-point of at least two extended conceits. Such
borrowing or adapting of Shakespeare's playful analogies is more
clearly seen in a passage of Donne's *Elegy IX, The Autumnal*, which
develops its metaphysical line of thought from Shakespeare's fanciful account of the 'pretty dimple' in Adonis's cheek (*Venus and Adonis*,
242–7):

    Love made those hollows, if himself were slain,
    He might be buried in a tomb so simple;
        Foreknowing well if there he came to lie,
        Why, there Love lived, and there he could not die.
    These lovely caves, these round enchanting pits,
    Opened their lovely mouths to swallow Venus' liking.

By comparing the dimple to a tomb, to caves and pits, Shakespeare
prefigures the kind of strained analogy typical of Donne; but in a
context of courtly feeling—'lovely', 'enchanting'—which softens
and modifies the sense of striking unfamiliarity. When Donne treats
the same idea in *The Autumnal* he makes the comparisons bluntly, forcing us to acknowledge their oddity and the deviousness of his wit
(ll. 13–18):

    Call not these wrinkles graves: if graves they were,
        They were Love's graves, for else he is nowhere.
    Yet lies not Love dead here, but here doth sit
        Vowed to this trench, like an anachorit;   [anchorite]
    And here, till hers—which must be his death—come,
    He doth not dig a grave, but build a tomb.

Like Adonis's dimple, Lady Herbert's wrinkles are seen as a tomb;
but only after Donne has suggested four times that they are graves,
and has transformed the figure of dead Love into a living hermit un-
comfortably confined in a trench: a pointedly unromantic notion.
Unlike Shakespeare, Donne makes no attempt to clothe his odd ideas
in appealing terms: his language is bare and uncompromising, and
in the absence of poetic decoration his argument stands out as a
hard plain structure. As a result, the whole sense of the passage
is dominated by Donne's wit, which does not so much play with a
charming conceit, as Shakespeare does—'Love made those hollows'—

as hammer out a strenuous pattern of ideas; beginning with a forth-right injunction, 'Call not these wrinkles graves', and qualifying its own conclusions as the argument thrusts forward, following the twists of the poet's mind. If Lady Herbert's wrinkles were graves, they must be the graves of Love: but Love is by no means dead, he lives in her wrinkles like a hermit in a cell, and will do so until she dies and those wrinkles become his tomb. Once Donne has fastened on to the central idea of considering the wrinkles graves, he clings to it tenac-iously, wringing out every bizarre consequence that the image can be made to yield. It is this intense intellectual working of a single concept which distinguishes Donne's handling of the idea first treated by Shakespeare, whose appeals to sensation—'pretty dimple' and 'opened their mouths'—find no parallel in Donne's forceful argu-ment. The difference in feeling between the two passages is implicit in their central ideas: the bewitching and youthful dimple, and the unromantic brand of old age.

If the comparison reveals how abruptly Donne broke away from the line of richly sensational poetry followed by Shakespeare, it also suggests how far this movement of dissent was prompted by a ten-dency which Donne found in the main stream of Elizabethan poetry. The essential novelty of his writing lay in what it left out: in its isolating of the intellectual element which in Shakespeare was combined with what may conveniently be called poetry of feeling. Donne made this isolated element of wit the dominating force of his writing. He pared down the abundant language of Elizabethan poetry to a comparatively narrow measure, discarding terms whose imaginative overtones would blur the clear, hard statement of the ideas which he struggles to define; and he sacrificed attributes of poetry which other writers would have considered indispensable—melody, courtly grace, mythological enrichment—in order to con-centrate upon the intellectual argument or demonstration which his poems habitually work out. Shakespeare too can devote himself to the kind of playful dialectic which proves the truth of paradox (*Venus and Adonis*, 1015–20):

> O love, quoth she, how much a fool was I,
> To be of such a weak and silly mind
> To wail his death who lives, and must not die
> Till mutual overthrow of mortal kind?
>> For he being dead, with him is beauty slain;
>> And beauty dead, black Chaos comes again.

But the argument is offered with too little energy to be intellectually impressive: Shakespeare knows that his paradox rests precariously on a form of words, and submits it as an amusing trifle. When Donne treats the same paradox in *A Nocturnal upon St Lucy's Day* he goes far beyond Shakespeare in hyperbole; but he develops his argument with such single-minded deliberateness that we might accept what he says as the expression of profound personal feeling (ll. 28–37):

But I am by her death, which word wrongs her,
Of the first nothing the elixir grown.
　　Were I a man, that I were one
　　I needs must know: I should prefer,
　　　　If I were any beast,
Some ends, some means: yea, plants, yea, stones detest
And love: all, all some properties invest.
If I an ordinary nothing were,
As shadow, a light and body must be here.
But I am none; nor will my sun renew.

Both language and structure of this passage are determined by
its intellectual purpose, which is to prove—absurdly, as it might
seem—that Donne has no existence. This argument is in itself a
manifestation of wit far more striking than Shakespeare has attempted, and Donne's passing references to points of scientific
belief—the first nothing, the elixir, the properties of plants and
stones—give particular emphasis to the intellectual standpoint of
his poem. Where another poet would use images to evoke feeling,
Donne brings in allusions to cosmology and natural philosophy to
resolve his ideas more sharply. He is not a man, nor an animal; he
is not even a plant or a stone, but nothing; even less than the nothing
of a shadow that is cast by a solid object. As he presses forward
his fantastic thesis, these references to contemporary belief help to
concentrate attention upon his ideas, where imagery drawn from
the realm of feeling would diffuse it over a wider field of interest.

Colloquial energy

It is probably for this reason that Donne uses conventional images
so seldom, preferring to express himself in vigorous, undecorated
language whose emotional impact is brought about by its colloquial
directness. The speaker seems to make no concessions to formal literary style, but to blurt out his feelings with the choking impatience or
excitement of a man too deeply absorbed in his private experience to
impose discipline upon what he writes. The actuality of emotional
engagement is there, in the rough language and uneven phrasing of
protest or passionate statement, where any considered literary effect
would immediately lower the temperature of his utterance:

'Tis true, 'tis day: what though it be?
O wilt thou therefore rise from me?
Why should we rise because 'tis light?
Did we lie down because 'twas night?

Break of Day, which opens with these lines, warns us not to assume that Donne is always writing about his actual experience, for here the speaker is a woman.

The *Songs and Sonets* are not poetry of spontaneous impulse, as the frequent elaborateness of their stanza-form makes clear; but they are poems written to create an effect of actual happening in the world of common fact. In this respect Donne dissociates himself from general Elizabethan practice very sharply. It is not his disrespectful rebuke to the sun in *The Sun Rising* that makes this poem so surprising, but Donne's emphatic rejection of the studied idiom reserved for poetry. The opening lines of Shakespeare's Sonnet 33 are typical of the formal literary manner by which the poet indicates the noble elevation of this theme. He is not attempting to describe the actual world, but to transmute a commonplace experience in the way that Sidney suggests, by turning its base metal to gold:

> Full many a glorious morning have I seen
> Flatter the mountain-tops with sovereign eye,
> Kissing with golden face the meadows green,
> Gilding pale streams with heavenly alchemy.

The creative power of the poet is made to work the same change upon its subject matter as the 'heavenly alchemy' of the sun upon the pallid landscape. It brings about this transformation by using language and forms of speech that have almost nothing in common with the spoken English of popular life. The opening phrase 'full many', used for 'several', tells us at once that the poet is adopting a manner too lofty to accept terms of popular speech. The outburst of feeling that begins *The Sun Rising* (lines 1–8) has just the opposite effect:

> Busy old fool, unruly sun,
> Why dost thou thus
> Through windows and through curtains call on us?
> Must to thy motions lovers' seasons run?
> Saucy pedantic wretch, go chide
> Late schoolboys, and sour prentices;
> Go tell court huntsmen that the king will ride;
> Call country ants to harvest offices.

In these eight lines only 'pedantic' falls outside the idiom of spoken English so convincingly represented in the phrasing of Donne's sentences. From the outset we are firmly placed in a familiar, everyday context of windows and curtains, schoolboys, apprentices and harvesters; where both language and forms of speech are irrevocably linked with common human feelings and experience. Where Shakespeare abounds in metaphor, 'flatter the mountain-tops . . . kissing the meadows', Donne speaks directly and with an entirely literal purpose: his windows and curtains are not part of a poetic analogy but objects taken from real life. The whole character of his poem is directed by a desire to represent the actuality of passionate experience. With this intention Donne refuses to employ the forms of poetic ornament which most Elizabethan writers adopted as a matter of course, limiting himself to a kind of basic English vocabulary which renders impressions in terms as stark as the grave-digger's discovery: 'a bracelet of bright hair about the bone'. This famous line from *The Relic* epitomizes Donne's power of making direct statement act upon the reader with the dramatic effect of figurative speech. Alliteration gives the phrase the emphasis of heightened feeling, but this is the only literary device which Donne uses here. He relies upon the force of plain colloquial terms to evoke an impression of sensational contact as sharp and immediate as a physical blow, which makes the discovery of the relic happen to the reader.

This may explain why, when Donne uses figurative expressions, he draws images and comparisons most readily from the field of science and allied studies. It would be mistaken to think of Donne simply as an Elizabethan highbrow or intellectual, for although his learning and intelligence are indisputable, his poetry is clearly the writing of a deeply passionate man. The so-called metaphysical images which are taken to characterize him are not designed to show his learning, and do not in fact represent any unusual degree of erudition. Any literate Elizabethan knew something about the celestial spheres, human anatomy, America and the nature of angels; though he may not have been accustomed to seeing these subjects referred to in love poetry. Donne brings in allusions to science and theology because he is trying to reach a state of finality or absoluteness through his writing, and because points of scientific belief are more helpful than natural images in such a task. This aim of reaching a condition of fixed security is most easily recognized in the closing lines of some of Donne's best known poems: *The Sun Rising*, for instance, (lines 29–30).

> Shine here to us, and thou art everywhere;
> This bed thy centre is, these walls thy sphere.

The same impression of complete resolution is evoked by the closing statement of *A Nocturnal upon St Lucy's Day*, (line 45) as the poem settles into the immobility of grief:

>   This
> Both the year's, and the day's, deep midnight is.

A more familiar example occurs in the final stanza of the *Hymn to God the Father* (lines 15–18) which is generally accepted as Donne's last poem, when the poet stills his disquiet and rests in the assurance of divine grace:

> Swear by thyself that at my death thy sun
>   Shall shine as it shines now and heretofore;
>   And having done that, thou hast done:
>   I have no more.

These poems end in the resolution of a spiritual or intellectual problem which Donne has announced at the outset. There is no need to remark that this process of working out some form of puzzle, or of proving a paradox, is highly characteristic of Donne; for it is the argumentative scheme of his poems which does most to justify their being called metaphysical. As exercises in logical reasoning they are usually very faulty, and the means by which Donne develops and rounds off his argument displays more wit than respect for dialectical method. 'On a round ball', he remarks in *A Valediction of Weeping*, (lines 11–16):

A workman that hath copies by, can lay
An Europe, Afric, and an Asia,
And quickly make that which was nothing, all.
  So doth each tear
  Which thee doth wear,
A globe, yea world, by that impression grow.

The argument only seems logically connected: an unmarked globe is not nothing, and does not become 'all' when the continents are engraved on it; nor do the lover's tears become worlds when they hold an image of his mistress. Donne knows this well enough, but his poetic impulse can only be satisfied when it has presented its ideas in the form of an argued demonstration. However far from logical truth in fact, he must seem to follow, step by step, a process of thought leading from initial thesis to final proof; and to a greater or lesser degree his poems fit themselves to this argumentative form.

We may suppose that Donne imposed this character upon his work because it suited his bent of mind, or because it gave the fullest play to his wit; but more probably the sense of proving and demonstrating which the poems communicate is a condition which Donne felt imaginatively impelled to create. As the colloquial directness of his language gives his poetry the sense of actual happening, and of an immediate contact with reality, so his dialectic seems to confirm the impression of solid truth which such familiar and spontaneous speech evokes. Donne's writing is perhaps to be understood as an attempt to make out of poetry a form of imaginative reality more positive and secure than Donne found in the world about him. His personal life was assailed by doubts and troubling uncertainties which seem only to have been temporarily stilled by marriage. His poetry is his answer to the insecurity which dogged him: an imaginative making of the dependable reality which he needed for peace of mind, and whose absence impelled him to create this synthetic equivalent.

It is important to reach some understanding of the private motives which urged Donne to write and which determined his style, for through this understanding we recognize that the curious 'metaphysical' features of his poetry are not modish decoration but an essential means of expression. The involved, sometimes almost tortured working-out of attitudes and relationships, the strained analogies and uneven rhythm which characterize his writing are an integral part of its meaning: a reflection of the mind labouring to organize the incoherent matter of private experience into systematic order, and to give the world of feeling a structure as positive and constant as a Euclidian demonstration. No poem can be represented by a paraphrase of its explicit sense, for part of its total effect on the reader is brought about by the unperceived working of rhyme and metre upon his feelings, and still more by a mysterious chemistry of words. This is especially true of Donne. His style seems at first gratuitously noisy and conspicuous, distracting attention from the substance of his poem to its mere manner of delivery or its oddities of thought. Later we come to realize how much of Donne's meaning is carried by what we had mistaken for superficial effects. The experience which he communicates to us is represented in large part by the almost physical difficulties of realizing ideas; by a laboured process of working-out and resolving which we are made to feel directly through disturbed patterns of speech and rough word-sounds. Donne's reference to climbing in a famous passage of *Satire III* (lines 79–82) shows how forcefully such effects contribute to the plain sense of his comment:

> On a huge hill,
> Cragged and steep, Truth stands; and he that will
> Reach her, about must and about must go,
> And what the hill's suddenness resists, win so.

Both metrically and in syntax the sentence is broken into disjointed phrases, which join the aspirates of 'huge hill' to represent the difficulties of approaching Truth. The word-sounds are unmusical throughout, and the irregular stressing—felt particularly in the unstressed rhyme-word 'will'—denies the passage all sense of steady movement: the commentary seems to follow the climber as he heaves and scrambles breathlessly towards his goal, which he finally reaches in the climax, 'win so'.

This characteristic passage of Donne's writing shows how integral his mode of expression is to the sense of his poetry. If his ideas were expressed in some other form—more gracefully, with a steadier rhythmical pulse—they would no longer describe the experience which Donne seeks to define. The oddities of metaphysical style do not stand on top of an otherwise plain poem, like fantastic ornament set on an inconsequential building: they are the poem, which has been compelled to assume this strangely idiosyncratic form by the pressures urging Donne to create. For him, metaphysical style was not merely a natural means of expression. It was the only mode by which he could represent the sombre intellectual searching of his religious life, and the persistent effort of the lover to prove himself and his mistress fused into a single, self-contained world of being. With his successors, who formed a 'school' only in the loosest sense of the term, this was not so. Such a strongly individual style was bound to admit imitators,

who adopted what they could of Donne's manner without his justification. Donne wrote as he did because what he had to say could not
be expressed otherwise: his purpose determined his means. There
could be no school of Donne, for his style was a uniquely personal
instrument which could not serve the need of other poets. What they
took from him was at best a dilution of his racked and involved
manner, and more usually a domesticated form of the conceit which
missed the inner logic of Donne's bizarre parallels, and offered
instead mere quaintness. Rather than being integral to the general
style of their poems, these metaphysical effects stand out like plums
in a cake; and their literary context derives not from Donne but
from Jonson.

The significance of Ben Jonson

Though a much less talented poet, Jonson far more than Donne set
English poetry on a new course, and by the end of the seventeenth
century had proved himself an innovator of deep and lasting influence. Unlike Donne—or indeed, most other Elizabethan poets of
moment—Jonson declared his literary standards in a small body of
critical writings, and preached these ideas to the group of young
poets who accepted him as master. Some of the most trenchant of his
critical comments are directed against the popular drama, whose
romantic excesses Jonson felt to be ludicrous and unworthy of
serious art:

> To make a child, now swaddled, to proceed
> Man, and then shoot up in one beard and weed
> Past threescore years, or, with three rusty swords
> And help of some few foot-and-half-foot words
> Fight over York and Lancaster's long jars.
>
> *Every Man in his Humour, Prologue, 17*

His own plays are usually set in the London of his own times, with
characters drawn from common life; and by observing the Unities
Jonson does still more to limit attention to a credible everyday
world, and the 'deeds and language such as men do use'. His comments, some directed almost explicitly against Shakespeare, indicate
the strong bias towards classical restraint and disciplined expression
which marks Jonson's critical outlook in general. He speaks out
against the literary taste of his age as bluntly as he attacks the im-
plausible scope of the romantic drama. 'Now nothing is good that is
natural', he writes in *Discoveries*; 'Right and natural language seem
to have the least of wit in it; that which is writhed and tortured is
counted the more exquisite . . . No beauty to be had but in wresting
and writhing our own tongue. Nothing is fashionable till it be de-
formed; and this is to write like a gentleman'.

Many of the particular comments, and probably the critical inspira-
tion of *Discoveries*, come from Jonson's reading of the ancient Roman

authors whose work constituted the basis of classical criticism throughout the Renaissance and during the two following centuries. It was Jonson who made the first determined attempt to graft these classical principles upon the native tradition of English poetry, both by direct instruction and by the example of his own writing. He began to introduce Horatian standards and principles to English audiences at a time when native poetry was more vigorously individual and adventurous than in any previous age, and as much unlike the ideal advanced by Jonson as English writing has ever been until the present. Where it was wild and exuberant, he wished it to be restrained and urbane; where—as in Donne's poetry—it was intensely personal, Jonson argued for a measured detachment of feeling, and where Elizabethan writing at its greatest tended to be involved and dense with meaning, Jonson required it to be simple and clearly expressed. 'The chief virtue of a style is perspicuity,' he remarks in *Discoveries*, 'and nothing so vicious [defective] in it as to need an interpreter.' This axiom condemns a great deal of Shakespeare's most powerful dialogue as well as much of Donne's writing; and we shall not be surprised to hear Jonson's opinion that Shakespeare 'needed art', or that he admired Donne for two poems which are either more restrained or less agitated in metre and feeling than the others: 'His verses *The Lost Chain* he hath by heart, and that passage of *The Calm*, "That dust and feathers do not stir, all was so quiet"'. So Drummond of Hawthornden reported, after Jonson had visited him in 1619; and although we know the first poem as *Elegy XI*, and barely recognize his quotation as coming from *The Calm*, (lines 17–18):

> No use of lanterns; and in one place lay
> Feathers and dust, today and yesterday;

there is no reason to doubt the general truth of Drummond's report. Another of his guest's remarks on the current literary scene was the apparently irritated opinion that Donne 'for not keeping of accent deserved hanging': a comment which shows that Jonson could not be won over by the emotional dynamism of Donne's poetry when so great a dislocation of rhythmical structure was involved. Evidently Jonson was not prepared to concede that strong passion should display itself in the kind of metrical upheaval so often found in Donne. The poet was not to write for the private relief of discharging profound feeling, but was to use the disciplines of his art to mould impulse into a temperate and well-balanced statement. When the poet allowed his personal involvement to wrench and distort language, forcing words to bear more meaning than they could express in clear terms, he was debasing the standards of good writing. 'Our style should be like a skein of silk', he writes; 'to be carried and found by the right thread, not ravelled and perplexed; then all is a knot, a heap.'

By introducing Horatian standards under the very shadow of Shakespeare's greatness, Jonson was breaking with all the traditions of English writing and issuing a direct challenge to the strain of emphatic individualism that seems to run through Elizabethan poetry. Singling out Lyly, Spenser, Marlowe, Nashe and Donne as five of the most strikingly talented writers of the quarter-century which brought Shakespeare into prominence, we see how each fashioned for himself a uniquely personal style by which he is instantly marked out and identified. In his great comedies Jonson himself is no less distinctive, for one of his principal satirical weapons is language as rhetorically inflated or overloaded as he attacks in his criticism: merely by speaking, his victim makes himself ridiculous. In this way Jonson may have been satisfying a deep imaginative urge to write in the exuberantly personal style which as critic he opposed, yet without exposing himself to a charge of inconsistency. But in his non-dramatic poetry he provides a copybook example of the restrained, emotionally detached and lucid manner which his criticism recommends. His translations of Horace, which render the felicities of Latin with a homely bluntness, must interest us for their attention to the points of style which Jonson felt important—clarity, conciseness, and simplicity of language:

> The poplar tall he then doth marrying twine
>   With the grown issue of the vine;
> And with his hook lops off the fruitless race,
>   And sets more happy in the place;
> Or in the bending vale beholds afar
>   The lowing herds there grazing are;
> Or the pressed honey in pure pots doth keep
>   Of earth, and shears the tender sheep;
> Or when that autumn through the fields lifts round
>   His head, with mellow apples crowned,
> How—plucking pears his own hand grafted had,
>   And purple-matching grapes—he's glad!

The Praises of a Country Life, 9–20

This is neither great nor memorable poetry: it lacks the energy of committed writing, is cumbrously expressed, and in leaving nothing to suggestion or personal feeling it fails to excite more than passing interest. But Jonson is roughing out a new literary style which was not to reach its completely resolved development for another century, and in its earliest form this new tradition should interest us by its intentions rather than by its achievement.

The controlled vigour of his style is seen to better advantage in *To Penshurst*, the first of a number of seventeenth-century poems extolling a country house and its family, in which Jonson presents an idealized picture of life that is industrious, pious and humane: the moral positive which might stand behind the images of corruption and folly dominating his satire. The country estate is the hub of an innocent and harmless system of life, whose tenants show their master a dutiful respect which recalls an earlier and more settled social order (lines 48–56):

But all come in, the farmer and the clown,
And no one empty-handed, to salute
Thy lord and lady, though they have no suit.
Some bring a capon, some a rural cake,
Some nuts, some apples; some, that think they make
The better cheeses, bring 'em; or else send
By their ripe daughters, whom they would commend
This way to husbands, and whose baskets bear
An emblem of themselves in plum or pear.

Here the clarity of Jonson's writing is enriched by its frank appeal
to sensuous feeling; and although he loses none of the perspicuity
which he values as critic, he begins to communicate with his reader
through word-sounds and imaginative suggestions as well as by
explicitly stated ideas. His comment about the 'ripe daughters'

> whose baskets bear
> An emblem of themselves in plum or pear

fuses wit with a joyously realized image which sets young womanhood
in a context of warm and rounded maturity. But this sensuous expansion is unobtrusively controlled, and Jonson is not diverted from his
main task of praising Penshurst through these images of natural
abundance. A balance has been established between the appeal of
simple, evocative language—'the purpled pheasant with the speckled
side', 'the blushing apricot and woolly peach'—and the need to
give his poem the organization of a readily intelligible commentary,
on which the poet's private feelings do not obtrude. The phrase
describing the pheasant has a verbal richness akin to the effect of
metaphor, but is in fact closer to impersonal statement. Jonson is
showing the way to temper emotion to a conscious literary discipline,
and to shape poetry by the standards of a polite culture hitherto alien
to English writing.

Unlike Donne, whose style ceased to justify itself when it was
imitated, Jonson offered his fellow-poets literary precepts and a
manner of writing which he meant them to adopt. Because his style
was not a reflection of individual temperament but a considered
and impersonal literary form, it could serve other poets equally well;
and we are not surprised to find writers of the Caroline period
working within this new tradition and at no great distance from
Jonson's particular example. *To Penshurst* was imitated by several
poets* who either repeated or extended its idealized conception
of a contented, self-sufficient community practising the civilized virtues of hospitality and moderation, and paying respect to established customs which in the world at large were being progressively
eroded. Perhaps by the single example of this poem Jonson successfully implanted an idea of human culture which, although increasing-

---

*Thomas Carew, *To Saxham*; Andrew Marvell, *Upon Appleton House*, John Dryden, *To my
honoured kinsman John Driden of Chesterton*. The tradition extends to Pope's *Moral Essay IV*.

Penshurst Place.

ly at odds with the disturbed state of English society under Charles, continued to appeal to educated taste and to encourage attempts to realize its promise of quiet and well-ordered existence.

The promise was not to be effectively fulfilled until the early eighteenth century, when English social culture reached the point of urbane development which it had willed itself to achieve; but in literature at least the main form of this achievement had been clearly foreshadowed only a few years after Jonson's death in 1637, by the courtier and poet John Denham. In *Cooper's Hill*, one of the first topographical poems, he summed up the classical ideal of poetry in two couplets addressed to the Thames:

> O could I flow like thee, and make thy stream
> My great example, as it is my theme!
> Though deep, yet clear; though gentle, yet not dull;
> Strong without rage, without o'erflowing full.

In both idea and expression these lines look forward to Pope, whose most decisive work was to be written more than seventy years later. Behind Denham stands the unmistakable influence of Jonson, whose efforts to deflect the course of English poetry towards this classical tradition of lucid, concise, forceful yet well-disciplined writing were now beginning to yield fruit.

Jonson had not been alone in wishing to curb the flamboyance and excess so characteristic of the Elizabethan spirit, and which in his eyes marred even the work of Shakespeare. At the time when Jonson was censuring popular taste, and trying to wean audiences away from their romantic diet of freaks and drolleries, a new and severe architectural style was announcing a similar break with the elaborate and overloaded tradition then current. The great houses built in the closing decades of Elizabeth's reign offer suggestive parallels in form and feeling with the prevailing literary style. They are majestically formal, enriched with architectural conceits of every kind, and dressed in a visual rhetoric so elaborate that we may wonder whether the imposing façade overlies any genuine purpose, or is itself its *raison d'être*. Inigo Jones, an architect who worked with Jonson in designing court masques, helped to introduce a completely different building style which seems even more in advance of its times than Jonson's innovations in poetry. The Queen's House at Greenwich and the Banqueting House at Whitehall, both built during the lifetime of Donne, impose the same kind of ordered restraint upon architectural form and decoration as Jonson was bringing to literary practice. Emphasis passes from ornament to structure: architectural features are relieved of the elaborations which smothered them and redefined in strong outline. Where the great Elizabethan houses might lead us to expect their inhabitants to be splendid yet curious half-mythical creatures, the new style reduces both the scale and the ostentatiousness of Elizabethan architecture to a point where simple human associations replace grandeur and display. Jonson praises

The frontispiece of Hatfield House, 1611.

Penshurst, with its medieval hall, for its lack of flamboyance; and ends his poem by suggesting that Penshurst is above all a home and not an empty showpiece (lines 99–102):

> Now, Penshurst, they that will proportion thee
> With other edifices, when they see
> Those proud ambitious heaps, and nothing else,
> Will say their lords have built, but thy lord dwells.

Marvell addresses the same compliment to Fairfax in *Upon Appleton House*, (lines 3–4) condemning the arrogance of architects who

> unto caves the quarries drew,
> And forests did to pastures hew;

and refusing to apologize for the unpretentiousness of the house which the great soldier has chosen for his retirement (lines 61–4):

> And yet what needs there here excuse,
> Where everything does answer use?
> Where neatness nothing can condemn,
> Nor pride invent what to contemn?

The poet judges the architect's work by standards which he observes in his writing; but even a cursory acquaintance with native building style during the reign of Charles will show how completely the characteristic opulence and lavishness of high Elizabethan architecture had fallen out of fashion. The change can be appreciated particularly well by comparing the frontispiece of Hatfield House, built in 1611, with the north range of Kirby Hall in Northamptonshire, which is dated 1640. The contrast between the self-assertive splendour of the older building and the graceful reserve of the other indicates not merely a shift of fashion but a growth of civilized awareness, which was not limited to any single field of human activity.

Jonson's literary principles, and the example of his writing, made a ready appeal to the young courtiers and intelligentsia—the 'mob of gentlemen', as Pope was to describe them—who wrote much of the minor poetry of his age. English society was becoming increasingly conscious of divisions and differences within itself, and not least in the literary tastes of the courtly and middle classes. Shakespeare, it is often observed, addressed himself to a compound audience made up of all classes and callings. This is less true of his last plays, which incline towards the tastes of a more discerning clientèle, and appeal to the gentler feelings of an audience able to pay for seats in the private theatres. Beaumont and Fletcher, his immediate successors, widened the gap between courtly and popular by writing almost exclusively for this new audience, which evidently expected its finer sensibilities to be brought into play. For his part, Jonson made the mistake of presenting to popular audiences plays both unfamiliar in genre and intellectually over their heads. The disappointment of failure prompted him to condemn popular taste outright, and to look

The Caroline Façade of Kirby Hall, 1640.

for appreciation only from the cultured and discriminating readers who could recognize his worth. Predictably, he found his disciples among the young gentlemen who shared his educated background, and who were pleased to prove their courtly credentials by adopting a literary style so distinct from the native tradition which popular taste approved.* By embracing Jonson's Horatian manner they identified themselves with the courtly society to which they looked for employment or preferment.

But accepting Jonson did not necessarily involve rejecting Donne, even though Donne probably offended more of Jonson's critical principles than any other important writer of the age. In his impudence and wit as a love poet, Donne made a powerful appeal to the same body of young writers. He too was a minority poet, barely known outside the circle of readers with access to manuscript copies of his work; and the markedly intellectual character of his poetry must have limited its appeal very severely outside this special audience. This could only have increased its attractiveness to its devotees. Jonson might persuade his young disciples to avoid Donne's roughness and to organize their writing on a firm and lucid structure, but not annul the fascination of his wit; in particular of the conceit. The result was a literary compromise. The poets of Jonson's 'tribe' followed his lead in the general matter of poetic style, producing well-turned verse whose easy negligence was to earn Pope's slight, and adding a courtly form of the conceit for an effect of intellectual elegance. Carew's inscription for the tomb of Lady Mary Wentworth, who died aged eighteen, includes a typical example of this blending of influences within a manner that is essentially courtly. The first stanza has the neatness of idea and expression which Jonson urged:

> And here the precious dust is laid,
>   Whose purely tempered clay was made
> So fine that it the guest betrayed.

The compliment is unobtrusive and deftly managed, served by a wit which gives polish to the sentiment. The second stanza develops this idea by offering an alternative explanation of the lady's early death, and at once Carew loses his balanced manner in pursuing an intellectual conceit:

> Else the soul grew so fast within,
>   It broke the outward shell of sin,
> And so was hatched a cherubin.

The image betrays Carew's readiness to re-use conceits brought about in another poet's struggle to realize his ideas. The passage of Donne's *Second Anniversary* (lines 179–184) from which Carew has borrowed his conceit allows us to watch Donne working towards the idea, which then comes about as the natural climax of a train of thought dominated by the notion of release:

*The so-called 'tribe of Ben' included Suckling, Carew, Randolph and Herrick.

But think that Death hath now enfranchised thee;
Thou hast thy expansion now, and liberty:
Think that a rusty piece, discharged, is flown
In pieces, and the bullet is his own
And freely flies. This to thy soul allow:
Think thy shell broke, think thy soul hatched but now.

Donne represents the process of excogitation, and his conceit of a
soul hatching out forms an organic part of his argument: Carew, on
the other hand, produces the idea out of nowhere, and cannot make
it integral to his poem. Transplanted from its native setting in *The
Second Anniversary*, its function becomes mainly decorative; and thus
what appears at first sight to be a metaphysical poem merely simulates
the process of thinking so vital to the character of Donne's writing,
offering instead an inert conceit transferred from its living context.

The school of Donne and the school of Jonson

Such borrowing and imitation of Donne's ideas continued throughout the seventeenth century, as lesser poets associated themselves with
the line of wit which he had initiated. Of Donne's courtly imitators
it might be said at once that the habitual clarity and ease of their
writing showed how little genuine need they felt to express themselves
through the involved arguments and abstruse analogies that were
natural to Donne. Their aim was to produce a metaphysical effect:
to amuse and perhaps to astonish by the sheer outlandishness of
ideas and comparisons, but without taxing the understanding of their
readers. Thus Lovelace begins a poem to his mistress's glove, 'Thou
snowy farm with thy five tenements', Marvell describes the flowers
at Appleton House as musketeers discharging volleys of scent, and
Crashaw, writing of Mary Magdalene's tears, suggests that in heaven

Where the milky rivers creep,
Thine floats above, and is the cream.

Unless the poet's intention were simply to advertise his ingenuity,
such imagery would be self-defeating, for it distracts attention from
the subject to the sheer oddity of the comparison. Donne is perhaps
hardly less bizarre when he sums up man as 'a province packed up
in two yards of skin'; but his image justifies itself both by his energy
of expression and by the imaginative recognition which it compels
the reader to share. We have no grounds for rejecting a poet's curious
account of his experience unless his writing fails to persuade us that
he is representing it truly; and most of Donne's successors are clearly
trying to heighten the interest of a commonplace event or perception
by forcing alien associations upon it. When Donne brings heterogeneous ideas together, he shows us why or how his mind has discovered their hidden likeness. The analogies of the *Hymn to God my
God* may strike us absurdly farfetched (lines 6–9):

> Whilst my physicians by their love are grown
>   Cosmographers, and I their map, who lie
> Flat on this bed, that by them may be shown
>   That this is my South-West discovery;

but later the inner logic of Donne's argument persuades us to accept his extraordinary point of view. The attitude of his doctors, watching intently for any change in his condition, suggests the complete absorption of cosmographers bent over their maps; and after making this visual comparison Donne clinches the analogy by arguing that his death will provide the issue from 'these straits' into the Pacific Sea of everlasting life. These conceits are the basis of his poem, which could not exist without them. It is a proper question whether his imitators, whose conceits float on the surface of their poems as witty embellishment, should be described as metaphysical poets.

Some reservations have to be made in this general criticism. Some forms of human experience are in themselves bizarre and unaccountable, and during the second quarter of the seventeenth century awareness of oddity and enigma beyond the range of normal understanding seems to have quickened; as though in protest at the growth of more rational trends of thought. Browne is perhaps an example of a writer who deliberately encouraged himself to become lost in spiritual and intellectual puzzles; but some of his contemporaries may have verged upon a kind of genuinely mystic insight such as poets would not undergo again until the Romantic Revival. Marvell is one of them. A man of unusually alert intelligence, he occasionally writes as though he had been taken off his guard by a sense of an indefinable power in the natural world, which immobilized his reason. The word 'green' recurs in his poems as a term whose charged significance has an almost mesmeric effect on his mind. When he describes himself plunging through the meadows at Nun Appleton, where the summer grass is ready for mowing, he admits a sense of awed incomprehension that is only half playful. In the great gulf of greenery his rational intelligence is drowned, and looking up in his abasement he sees the giant insects crowing over him from remote spires of grass, far above his head (*Upon Appleton House*, lines 369–376):

> And now to the abyss I pass
> Of that unfathomable grass,
> Where men like grasshoppers appear;
> But grasshoppers are giants there.
> They, in their squeaking laugh, contemn
> Us as we walk more low than them;
> And, from the precipices tall
> Of the green spires, to us do call.

While Marvell's intelligence is offering a witty commentary on the quaintness of his rural experience, his deeper feelings are stirred by the huge vitality of the grass which engulfs and dwarfs him. His phrase 'that unfathomable grass' is at once bantering and serious; for although Marvell merely pretends that the grass rises high above him in 'precipices tall', its silent energy presents a puzzle which his mind cannot deal with. What he senses or half-sees in the natural world is an overwhelming and single-minded force of growth which, if not actually threatening man, challenges his domination of the earth.

The occasional hints of quasi-mystic experience in Marvell's poetry justify some of his odder conceits, which are not always prompted by the kind of fantastic wit which sees the fishers with their coracles as 'Antipodes in shoes'. An element of strangeness had shown itself in metaphysical poetry from the outset, and continued to dominate the style. This tendency to explore and examine the less familiar aspects of man's relationships and environment might have made it inevitable that the more serious developments of metaphysical poetry should be in the field of devotional writing, both verse and prose. What the Cavalier poets took from Donne was used as a superficial adornment of their work, whose subject was generally love or courtly affairs. The successors of Donne who deserve to be described as metaphysical poets in a strict sense of the term left the imitation of his amorous manner to others, and followed—at a respectful distance—the example of his devotional verse.

Yet here too there is a marked disparity between the work of master and disciple; and if we are to speak of a school of Donne we must be clear about the extent of the influence we are claiming for him. Donne's poetry, of whatever kind, is shaped on the anvil of an individual temperament which changes very little between the relentless arguments of the *Songs and Sonets* and the tortured rhetoric of the *Holy Sonnets*. It is intensely personal writing, and no follower could have hoped to produce poetry of any value by imitating the idiosyncrasies of style which reflect Donne's turbulent feelings, and his straining efforts to secure himself against spiritual doubt. A true successor of Donne would find just as personal a manner of expression. He might not share the anxiety which impels much of Donne's finest devotional poetry; and writing which reflected a calmer and more assured mind might not readily be recognized as metaphysical at all. In respect of George Herbert, who has some clear right to be acknowledged as Donne's pupil, this is just the case. The quality of his work is most readily appreciated from a comparison with Donne. The opening lines of *Holy Sonnet IX* are immediately typical of the dramatizing of personal alarm which sounds so frequently in Donne's restless colloquies with God:

> If poisonous minerals, and if that tree
> Whose fruit threw death on else immortal us,
> If lecherous goats, if serpents envious
> Cannot be damned, alas, why should I be?

The lines are clamorous with ill-concealed terror, which accumulates

through a series of jarring phrases until it bursts in the climactic
'Alas' and the rebellious protest, 'Why should I be?' The uneven
rhythms of the passage reflect Donne's disturbed spirit, which has
twisted language into the painfully knotted phrase 'else immortal us'.
There are no concessions to musical effect, but an outspoken bluntness of reference which supplements the impression of a passionate
outburst of feeling. No poem of Herbert's matches this roughness and
violence of expression, and *The Collar* is perhaps the only work of his
which recalls, even distantly, the mood of angry protest so typical of
Donne. Herbert too can challenge God to reveal his purposes, which
seem designed to frustrate and disappoint those who serve him:

> Shall I be still in suit?
> Have I no harvest but a thorn
> To let me blood, and not restore
> What I have lost with cordial fruit?
> Sure there was wine
> Before my sighs did dry it: there was corn
> Before my tears did drown it.
> Is the year only lost to me?
> Have I no bays to crown it?
> No flowers, no garlands gay? all blasted,
> All wasted?

This extract from *The Collar* (lines 6–16) resembles the opening lines
of *Holy Sonnet IX* in its questioning of God's purposes, but the likeness
goes no further. Where Donne is clamorous, Herbert is plaintive and
a little wistful; and both the finer craftsmanship and the quieter movement of his poem suggest that his feelings allow him to present a more
considered piece of writing than Donne's passionate urgency makes
possible. Perhaps because *The Collar* does not convey such an impression of a sudden outburst of raw feeling we are less easily
convinced that Herbert's complaints have any comparable basis:
when he admits

> Sure there was wine
> Before my sighs did dry it

we know that there will be wine again. Even in this unusually troubled
poem, Herbert's verse retains the characteristically dulcet quality
which makes it difficult to believe that his spiritual misgivings trouble
him very deeply. His language may have an artless simplicity, but we
cannot feel—as we so often do with Donne—that he is speaking out of
the experience itself, without reflecting about the terms he uses.
Herbert picks his words with care, and with a very clear conception of
the literary effect which he intends to produce. Unlike Donne, he
habitually writes in the past tense, setting his crises of faith at some
distance, and bringing the reader to safe ground at the end of the
poem. We can suppose that he enjoyed a far greater sense of inward
security throughout his life than did Donne, for his family circum-

stances protected him against many of the strains which Donne suffered; and we should not expect his poetry to reflect any comparable distress of spirit. But the difference between the two men does not lie in the degree of spiritual disturbance expressed by each so much as in the kind of poetry which each wills himself to produce. Herbert's is the writing of a meticulous literary artist; and in this respect he owes more to Jonson than to Donne.

This quality in Herbert's work is most readily seen in its use of emblematic images. The bare terms of metaphysical argument are uncongenial to him, and his poems commonly develop through an account of some private experience. He prefers to express himself picturesquely, through figures which are partly emblems to be 'read' in the way that allegorical characters are interpreted. His question in *The Collar*,

> Have I no harvest but a thorn
> To let me blood?

involves an essentially pictorial mode of expression. The terms which Herbert has unexpectedly linked together—harvest, thorn, blood—derive most of their force from their function as religious emblems, 'thorn' and 'blood' having imaginative associations with the Agony which transform their everyday character. The reader is not made to think or to follow a connected argument, but to respond to the unspoken meaning behind these pictorial figures. What seems at first reading to be uncontrived and almost naively expressed is in fact written with a good deal of sensitive artistry. Its simpleness of feeling and vocabulary reflect Herbert's literary purpose, and not his private background, which before he became a country priest had been a mixture of university and court. The cultivated pietism of his writing is in effect a courtly mode, appealing to the heart rather than to the mind, and seeking to move tender feelings by the note of wistful regret or wan bravery which Herbert strikes so frequently:

> I gave to Hope a watch of mine; but he
>   An anchor gave to me.
> Then an old prayer-book I did present;
>   And he an optic sent.   [magnifying-glass]
> With that I gave a vial full of tears;
>   But he a few green ears.
> Ah, loiterer! I'll no more, no more I'll bring:
>   I did expect a ring.

This concise, highly characteristic poem exemplifies Herbert's style and manner in many ways. It is charming and a little inconsequential, but put together with a craftsman's skill and delicacy. Its emblems of watch, anchor, prayer-book and the others are homely and picturesque, and present only a mild intellectual puzzle: it does not need much mental effort to realize that the watch represents impatience, the anchor constancy and the ring a state of union with God. The emblems

have a pleasant oddity which give the poem some metaphysical likeness, but their pictorial function asserts itself more strongly: Herbert
is again thinking in visual images rather than in intellectual terms, and
the poem makes its point by its appeal to feeling. Its short lines
represent the poet's repeated disappointment, and the two closing
lines bring the poem to a climax of emotional frustration which is also
its natural conclusion. We do not take this very seriously: his angry
'no more, no more I'll bring' suggests the hurt indignation of a child
who will soon forget his disappointment and this hasty resolution.
Herbert knows this, and has fashioned a carefully wrought poem
about an engagingly minor experience; addressing himself to an
audience who will appreciate its sensitive workmanship and respond
to its wistful simplicity. Herbert may have cut himself off from the
world of sophisticated affairs, but his literary standards and outlook
remain those of a cultured society for whom stylistic grace is instinctive.

He is not always so distant from the forceful metaphysics of Donne.
Occasionally he shows himself capable of producing the 'strong lines'
which typify Donne's wrestling with ideas, and of forging analogies
that are as farfetched yet persuasive as we expect of good metaphysical
poetry. The second stanza of *The Agony* (lines 7–12) reveals this more
powerful aspect of Herbert:

> Who would know Sin, let him repair
> Unto Mount Olivet: there shall he see
> A man so wrung with pains that all his hair,
>   His skin, his garments, bloody be.
> Sin is that press and vice which forceth pain
> To hunt his cruel food through every vein.

But despite the energy of the two last lines, this is not writing in the
tradition of Donne. In *Good Friday, riding Westward*, Donne makes himself a spectator of the Crucifixion and makes us feel the horror of
seeing the dying Christ. Herbert holds the Agony at a distance, and
offers a picture of Christ's suffering which evokes pathos by its
sensitively mannered account of pain. In the next stanza Herbert's
references to the Crucifixion show a still greater tendency to soften
the reality of torment and death, to the extent that bloodshed is made
to seem attractive (lines 13–18):

> Who knows not Love, let him assay
> And taste that juice which on the Cross a pike
> Did set again abroach: then let him say
>   If ever he did taste the like.
> Love is that liquour sweet and most divine,
> Which my God feels as blood, but I as wine.

The ideas of this stanza can be justified by the doctrine of transub-
stantiation; but in expressing them Herbert prompts a response which
not every reader will find agreeable. The communicant, Herbert im-

Good Hopes, *we best accomplish may,*
By lab'ring *in a* constant *Way.*

ILLVSTR. IX.   *Book.* 3

SOme Folkes there are, (and many men fuppofe,
That I my felfe, may paffe for one of thofe)
Who many likely Bufineffes intend,
Yet, bring but very few, unto an end.
Which folly to prevent, this *Emblem,* here,
Did in a luckie houre, perhaps, appeare.
For, as to draw a *Circle,* with our hand,
We caufe the brazen *Compaffes* to ftand
With one foot firmely fixed one the ground ;
And move the other in a *Conftant-round* :
Right fo, when we fhall purpofe to proceed
In any juft, and profitable deed,
We firft, fhould by a *conftant-refolution,*
Stand firme, to what we put in execution :

An emblem, from George Wither's Collection of Emblems, *1635.*

plies, is not drinking consecrated wine but the blood which runs down Christ's body, and relishing it like a connoisseur. As a metaphysical conceit, this suggestion anticipates some of the more extreme parallels of Crashaw's religious verse; and like them indicates how seriously the intellectual force and forthrightness of Donne's metaphysics have been weakened by yielding to a courtly taste for bizarre elegance and touching sentiment. Metaphysical poetry may have gained other attractions in this process, and whether Herbert is preferable to Donne is a matter of personal choice. The more important critical issue is whether even Herbert is to be judged 'metaphysical' in his poetic style, or whether his writing is impelled mainly by purposes to which the familiar features of Donne's style are subservient.

A particular style, we have seen, can only be entirely valid for the writer whose personality it reflects: for him it is not a way of writing but the only means of shaping a literary equivalent of himself. Something similar is true of a literary period. A mode of writing goes out of fashion when it ceases to represent current sensibility and outlook. As the transformation of architectural style suggests, between Elizabeth and Charles the temper of English life changed too radically for a single idiom to continue in force. Although we may be encouraged to regard Donne's metaphysical style as foreshadowing a 'new' scientific outlook, it is in fact highly characteristic of its period. However unlike Shakespeare in lesser respects, Donne declares himself with a rhetorical grandeur which identifies him as a poet of the same age. Even when he is most aware of man's sinful and corrupt state, he remembers that man is also God's last and most splendid piece of handiwork, and the centre about which the whole universal fabric moves. This position gives an importance to human experience which justifies Donne's intense intellectual curiosity about himself, and which demands language appropriate to man's giant stature. The Donne of the *Holy Sonnets* speaks with such an accent of greatness, as though the whole of cosmos were involved in his struggle with the demons of spiritual doubt. Herbert makes no attempt to echo this heroic voice. He speaks out of a smaller and more homely world on which the twilight seems to be falling; mildly reproachful in the face of treatment which he does not understand, and seldom allowing his protest to ruffle the composure of his writing:

> I got me flowers to straw thy way,
>   I got me boughs off many a tree;
> But thou wast up by break of day,
>   And brought'st thy sweets along with thee.
>   *Easter*, 1—4.

The flowers and sweets of this poem characterize the element of courtly grace in Herbert which belongs as much to his age as Donne's flamboyance to his. If, as Grierson suggested, metaphysical poetry was inspired by a philosophical conception of 'the role assigned to the human spirit in the great drama of existence', it would be unreasonable to expect poets of the Caroline period to produce such writing. The poetry of Herbert and Vaughan crystallizes a sense of lonely bewilderment and helplessness that cannot be associated with any great drama. They wrote when the age of heroic individualism was past, and in a language tempered to their quieter experience. What they took from Donne was limited to figures of style; for like the still greater poet of his age, Donne forged a means of expression which was both unmistakably characteristic of its times and an intimate reflection of himself.

5 A critical examination of some metaphysical poems: Donne to Marvell

John Donne

Woman's Constancy

Now thou hast loved me one whole day,
Tomorrow when thou leav'st, what wilt thou say?
Wilt thou then antedate some new-made vow,
   Or say that now
We are not just those persons which we were?
Or that oaths made in reverential fear
Of Love and his wrath any may forswear?
Or, as true deaths true marriages untie,
  So lovers' contracts, images of those,
10 Bind but till sleep, death's image, them unloose?
    Or, your own end to justify
For having purposed change and falsehood, you
Can have no way but falsehood to be true?
Vain lunatic, against these scapes I could   [*evasions*]
   Dispute and conquer, if I would;
   Which I abstain to do:
For by tomorrow I may think so too.

Donne's love poetry might be spoken by two entirely different characters. One is a lover almost oblivious of the outside world, assured by the knowledge of love returned by a woman—perhaps his wife—whose identity he feels himself to share. The other is a *roué* who scorns the Petrarchan poets' attempts to deify woman, and exposes the shameless motives of her behaviour with the acid wisdom of wide experience. Many readers like to assume that the most profoundly felt of the lover's poems were addressed to Ann More, either before or after marriage; and that the scandalously outspoken and cynical onslaughts upon woman reflect the young man-about-town whom Donne had been previously. But there is no need to suppose that either of these figures mirrors Donne himself; and good reason to regard the audacious cynic who speaks *Woman's Constancy* and *The Apparition* as a persona which Donne adopts in order to heighten the shock effect of his strikingly unconventional attitude.

    These two poems serve as showcase for the brilliantly inventive wit of a young poet bent upon proving his originality and intransigeance; which he does by addressing the mistress in blunt and unromantic terms, and by showing a practised understanding of her insincerity. She has loved him for a whole day—in itself a miracle—and must obviously soon find an excuse for dropping him. How will she justify her fickleness? By back-dating a promise to some new lover, or by explaining that she is no longer the person who swore fidelity yesterday? Or will she declare that oaths made under compulsion—of love—have no binding force: or again, will she argue that just as death dissolves marriage, so sleep—a seeming form of death—dissolves yesterday's contract of eternal love? Or finally, will she represent her falseness as truth, in that she never intended to be faithful, and so is being true to her original intention? At this point the poet thrusts her excuses aside with a contemptuous phrase: 'Vain lunatic!' If he thought it worth the trouble he would take up her arguments and disprove them all; but it would be labour wasted, for by tomorrow he may be ready to echo them.

It seems safe to assume that Donne was the first English poet to call his mistress a lunatic. By using this abusive term in the context of love poetry he shows how far he is prepared to challenge accepted ideas and practices. The mistress is not to be treated as a remote goddess: she is not even a convincing liar, and the lover dismisses her hypocritical excuses with a scornful insult. Instead of following tradition by begging her favours or extolling her beauty, he invents for her the kind of insincere apology which he knows she will presently offer him as she breaks her vows. These ingenious excuses are the most 'metaphysical' part of the poem, crediting the mistress with a very unlikely ability to justify her behaviour by a series of sophisms which in fact prove Donne's wit. But in suggesting that the mistress might herself concoct such utterly specious arguments, Donne is portraying woman in a guise which no Renaissance poet would normally have considered. Speaking as a cynical realist, he depicts her as fickle and calculating; using her cunning to wriggle out of an unwelcome situation, by arguing that yesterday's oath is no longer binding. In exposing her hypocrisy, the poet seems to be making a protest against such moral casuistry; but the poem has a sting in its tail. By tomorrow, he will himself be ready to echo these empty excuses, and just as relieved to part company with this mistress of a night. He has expected nothing better of her; and to deny the mistress any satisfaction he admits finally that it suits his purposes that she should prove such a plausible liar.

Although our first impression may be that Donne is making a vituperative attack upon woman, it would probably be more correct to see the poem as an impudently witty assault on a prevailing convention, in which Donne stands accepted manners and attitudes on their heads. The drily realistic assumption that, having loved him 'one whole day', the mistress must be on the point of leaving him, establishes at the outset how emphatically Donne rejects the current fashion in love poetry. There is to be no highminded idealism, no unsatisfied longing, no heartbroken despair, but a down-to-earth appreciation of deceitful motives and rapid disillusioning on both sides. This lover is no helpless victim of a fascinating mistress whose coldness or hauteur drives him out of his mind, but a cynically knowing analyst able to predict exactly how she will disengage herself from a contract that has quickly become wearisome. He exposes her without indignation or protest: his own love has been just as transient, and he is glad to be rid of her. For once she has met her intellectual match, a lover able to out-do her in fabricating elaborate excuses; and so for once the mistress and not the lover is worsted. Here again Donne asserts his aggressive originality.

In point of style, *Woman's Constancy* has many characteristic features of metaphysical poetry. It begins abruptly, without preparation or setting: the lover addresses the mistress and the reader is left to imagine the circumstances for himself. The language is unromantically plain and straightforward, mixing colloquial expressions such as 'one whole day' with a few legal terms—'antedate' and 'contract'—but excluding literary decoration. The tone is strenuous and unrelaxed. After the briefest of preliminaries, the speaker begins to fire a series of pointed questions which hammer upon the mistress, and give her no chance of recovering her shattered composure. Obviously he does not intend her to answer, if there were any way of throwing back his accusations. As though the opening words of the poem turn on an electric current or open a floodgate, we feel ourselves dazed like the lady by a bombardment of questions, which stops only so that Donne can deliver his *coup-de-grâce* by remarking that he too is ready to see their liaison dissolve. In this way the poem develops not the kind of lyrical atmosphere common to most love poetry, but a sense of controlled power whose masculine force proves itself in this devastating exposure and mockery of the woman's attempt to disguise her fickleness. This energy, bursting upon the reader with an effect almost like that of physical violence, is a vital feature of Donne's style.

The Apparition

When by thy scorn, O murd'ress, I am dead,
And that thou think'st thee free
From all solicitation from me,
Then shall my ghost come to thy bed,
And thee, feigned vestal, in worse arms shall see.
Then thy sick taper will begin to wink,
And he whose thou art then, being tired before,
Will, if thou stir or pinch to wake him, think
    Thou call'st for more,
10 And in false sleep will from thee shrink.
And then, poor aspen wretch, neglected thou
Bathed in a cold quicksilver sweat wilt lie,
    A verier ghost than I.
What I will say, I will not tell thee now
Lest that preserve thee; and since my love is spent,
I'd rather thou should'st painfully repent
Than by my threat'nings rest still innocent.*

The Apparition, another poem of seventeen lines, shows Donne making a still more pungent attack upon the conventions of romantic love. The vitriolic opening line, 'When by thy scorn, O murd'ress, I am dead,' respects Petrarchan tradition to the extent of accepting that the lover will die of unrequited love; but the stinging accusation, 'O murd'ress', carries a charge of contemptuous feeling that is wholly alien to the self-pitying mood of the hopeless Petrarchan lover. This is very much a live man's poem, and if he contemplates his death it is for the malicious pleasure of planning how he will torment the woman whose unkindness killed him. His promise of how he will haunt her involves some revelations far more damaging to the lady than the simple accusation of murder. 'Then shall my ghost come to thy bed,' the poet declares, 'And thee, feigned vestal, in worse arms shall see.' The phrase 'feigned vestal', set parenthetically so that it gathers emphasis, blots the lady's reputation by a single, exactly calculated stroke. She has refused herself to the poet as though prizing her virginity above everything, but at her bedside the ghost will see the truth: the professed chastity that is a mask for sexual looseness. If there could be any more damning accusation than this—or any suggestion further from the elevated spirit of Renaissance love poetry—it is that the lady is not very fussy about whom she chooses as her sexual partner; and this Donne asserts. This blunt reference to her actual taste and habits prepares the reader for the still more outspoken comments by which the poet compounds his defamation:

> And he whose thou art then, being tired before,
> Will, if thou stir or pinch to wake him, think
>   Thou call'st for more,
> And in false sleep will from thee shrink.

This unsparingly realistic satire strips sex of all romantic glamour, and presents the lady as a ridiculous figure. She is to be branded as a libertine, but denied the satisfaction of appearing in a rhapsodic account of sexual fruition: instead, she is set down squarely in the exhausted aftermath of love-making, with a lover now limp and mulishly unresponsive to what he mistakes for further demands. These unaccommodating references are not intended only to humiliate the lady, for clearly part of Donne's purpose is to startle his readers by treating a subject normally wrapped in richly evocative ideas with a down-to-earth detachment which sees things in their banal actuality. He remains firmly anchored to the real world, and both the lady and romantic convention suffer by being brought down to the level of commonplace experience.

Ignored by her sleepy and unchivalrous lover, the lady will have to face her terror alone, running with sweat and shaking like a leaf. If we took the poem literally, we should say that here Donne was find-

---

*The lover would prefer her to sin and be haunted rather than take his warning and remain constant and chaste.

ing compensation for his wounded feelings through a wild fantasy of revenge; but the wit and controlled venom of *The Apparition* do little to encourage this reading. With the line, 'A verier ghost than I,' Donne establishes his complete mastery of the situation, in a manner very similar to that of the previous poem, where he leaves the woman without a leg to stand on. Having broken her resistance, as before he now adopts a quieter tone, though the sense of his remarks remains maliciously cruel; and to complete her demoralization he declares that he has, in any case, already ceased to love her. We might object that, if this is so, the lover will not die of a broken heart and so he will have no occasion to haunt his mistress; but the notion of romantic death has served its purpose of setting in motion a poem designed to ridicule such conceptions. Here again there can be no question of believing that a lover who expressed his feelings with such energy and concentrated purpose could be in much danger of succumbing to blighted hopes. The driving power displayed in this poem and in *Woman's Constancy* underlies Donne's confidence as a literary revolutionary, overturning the established attitudes of his day. To this extent only we may regard these iconoclastic poems as parts of his autobiography. The simple dramatic situations which he invents, here a discarded lover burning with angry contempt against woman's guile, allow Donne to liberate his creative energy through a passage of invective; gratingly uncouth in idiom but designed with great intellectual subtlety.

Donne's subtlety does not strike us immediately, for the impact of his vigorously colloquial language distracts attention from other aspects of the poem. Later we find it easier to notice how unobtrusively the free-speaking commentary of the first five lines is organized into a sentence, to form a compact section of the story. The next five lines, from 'Then thy sick taper' to 'from thee shrink', make up a second sentence and the middle section of the story; so that while Donne appears to be writing informally and upon impulse, using the vocabulary and expressions of spoken English—'thou think'st thee free', 'being tired before', 'pinch to wake him'—he is in fact giving his poem the ordered shape that goes with craftsmanship. Unlike *Woman's Constancy*, this poem does not involve metaphysical argument or moral casuistry, but is a relatively straightforward piece of story-telling in advance; arranged upon the simple basis of 'When . . . then . . . and then', and culminating in the frightening prospect of what the ghost will say, which the speaker conceals. This development provides a framework firm enough to contain the explosive parentheses through which the lover gives relief to his overcharged feelings: 'O murd'ress', 'feigned vestal', and 'poor aspen wretch', and braces the poem against the malice which cuts and twists through it. Except in these interjections, the speaker does not show his suppressed anger and indignation, but adopts a silkily deliberate manner which hangs over words and phrases with a lingering enjoyment of the lady's rising panic. In the line, 'From all solicitation from me', the voice is made to pick out every syllable of the self-contemptuous term 'solicitation', which represents the lady's disparagement of his wooing. As he approaches the climax of his story the poet's pace does not quicken; and his pointing of the lines shows how unhurriedly he moves forward, savouring the sweetness of his revenge:

And in false sleep will from thee shrink.

This culminating line is uninterrupted but heavily accented; the spondee 'false sleep' being followed by three stressed words, 'from thee shrink', which give the promise a sense of absolute certainty. Donne is causing the event to happen through the power of his description, not to the lady but to the reader. The four lines ending in 'shrink' illustrate his remarkable ability to evoke a strong imaginative response through the use of entirely prosaic terms—here, monosyllabic words taken from common speech.

Elsewhere in *The Apparition* we find some characteristic use of images, where although Donne concedes something to metaphorical expression he does not lose his grasp upon literal facts. The line, 'Then thy sick taper will begin to wink,' calls up a visual impression of a dwindling flame; 'wink' having the sense of closing both eyes, and not only one. 'Sick taper' is a typically metaphysical image in its juxtaposing of seemingly unrelated ideas, though in fact an Elizabethan reader would have recognized a closer connection between 'sick' and 'taper' than would appear to us. The vital spirit of life was conceived to be a small flame within the body, and thus a guttering candle might indeed resemble a sick man approaching death. But the image is only half metaphorical, for while the adjective suggests other associations, the noun maintains the literal sense of Donne's reference. This is true of the two images which follow, 'poor aspen wretch' and 'cold quicksilver sweat'. The nouns are used literally, and each is qualified by an equally literal adjective—'poor', 'cold'—and by a figurative one. 'Aspen' involves an allusion to the natural world, rare in Donne; while 'quicksilver' has the typical unexpectedness of a metaphysical image, though its associations of beady, glistening and quick-moving droplets are splendidly matched to the notion of sweat breaking out all over the lady's body. The effect of this compromise between literal and figurative terms is to limit the scope of Donne's metaphor. He brings imagination into play, but does not allow it to distract attention from the actual object—the taper or the sweat—which he is referring to. In this way the intellectual element of his poem is made to dominate over its impulses towards imaginative impressionism, and the actuality of his subject is held firmly in view.

The Flea

Mark but this flea, and mark in this
How little that which thou deny'st me is:
It sucked me first, and now sucks thee,
And in this flea our two bloods mingled be.
Thou know'st that this cannot be said
A sin, nor shame, nor loss of maidenhead;
   Yet this enjoys before it woo,
   And pampered, swells with one blood made of two;
   And this, alas, is more than we would do.

10 O stay, three lives in one flea spare,
Where we almost, yea, more than married are!
This flea is you and I, and this
Our marriage-bed and marriage-temple is.
Though parents grudge, and you, we're met
And cloistered in these living walls of jet.
   Though use make you apt to kill me,
   Let not to that self-murder added be,
   And sacrilege, three sins in killing three.

Cruel and sudden, hast thou since
20 Purpled thy nail in blood of innocence?
Wherein could this flea guilty be
Except in that drop which it sucked from thee?
Yet thou triumph'st, and say'st that thou
Find'st not thyself nor me the weaker now.
   'Tis true: then learn how false fears be;
   Just so much honour, when thou yield'st to me,
   Will waste, as this flea's death took life from thee.

In *The Flea* this intellectual concentration is unremitting, and no side-issues offer even momentary relief from Donne's closely followed argument. Again his purpose is to establish his moral and intellectual mastery by refuting the mistress's reasons for keeping her virginity, and by proving the emptiness of her fears. His demonstration, argued over twenty-seven lines of sustained reasoning and outrageous sophistry, rolls inexorably over all her protests and finally reaches its irresistible conclusion that the loss of maidenhood is nothing more than a fleabite. The lady's case has been demolished as much by the sheer weight and resourcefulness of Donne's argument as by the reasons which he offers; and in the face of this defeat we must suppose that she can only surrender. There are of course no grounds for reading the poem as an indication of Donne's private morals, much less for supposing that it represents an argument used in some actual attempt at seduction. The witty point of *The Flea* lies in its preposterousness, not merely in the argument itself but in the tacit suggestion that the lady's resistance could be worn down by such means. Again Donne is proving his originality by turning convention upside down;

making it seem that women are won not by gifts, faithful service and loving speeches but by metaphysical proof that virginity is worthless.

The argument of the poem begins and ends with a fleabite. The insect has bitten the lover and the mistress in turn, and now contains a mixture of their bloods. Thus the flea has brought about the kind of union which the lover desires, yet without raising any moral protest from the mistress; enjoying them both with no longwinded preliminaries, and growing into a compound being as they might if the lady would yield to him. When she threatens to kill the flea, he restrains her: the insect is now them, filled with their two bloods. It is also the marriage-bed in which they were physically united, and the church in which their marriage was celebrated. Despite hostile parents and the lady's own reluctance, they have become a single being within the flea's body. Although, hardened by custom, she might think nothing of murdering part of him by killing the flea, that crime would involve suicide and sacrilege; for she would also kill part of herself and destroy the marriage-temple in which they were united. But she persists in her triple crime; and having 'purpled her nail' in the flea's blood she refutes his argument about murder and suicide by showing that neither of them is any weaker for having lost the particle of life supposedly sucked from them. In this momentary triumph she gives the lover the means of crushing her in a final, unanswerable demonstration by turning her own point against her. She is right, he admits; and just as she lost nothing of consequence to the flea, so in surrendering to him her honour will suffer no more than a fleabite.

The poem is a *tour-de-force* of irreverent wit, taking a trivial and utterly unromantic incident as the occasion of an exercise in fantastic ingenuity. Donne's suggestion that the flea represents both the united lovers, their marriage-bed and a marriage-temple, and that by squashing it the lady commits three grave crimes, is perhaps the most astonishingly contrived of all metaphysical conceits. The poem was no doubt partly impelled by a current fashion for writing elaborately learned treatises on things of no importance, which in 1579 had produced a book proving 'that baldness is much better than bushy hair'.* The close-knit structure of apparently serious argument which Donne erects on so minute a basis sets an example of witty nonsense which other Elizabethan writers might have despaired of rivalling. Yet however ludicrous his metaphysical disquisition on the flea and its multiple significance, Donne's argument succeeds in its purpose: the lady leaps in to point out the fault in his analogy, and so plays into his hands. Once again an inexorable process of reasoning, whose logical flaws contribute to the final triumph, has enabled this very unconventional lover to outwit the lady and to force his own terms upon her.

His disregard for convention appears most obviously in his frank desire for sexual intercourse. In poetry of the polite tradition which Donne pointedly rejects, the lover might approach the mistress as a

*Donne himself wrote a number of prose paradoxes with such titles as 'A Defence of Women's Constancy', 'That Women ought to Paint', and 'That a wise man is known by much Laughing'.

suppliant, but if he hoped to be granted this ultimate favour he did not hint that she might yield to him physically. Her chastity and good name were virtues which he was expected to honour, and his faithful service was to be impelled by respect for her beauty of mind and spirit, not by her attractive sexuality. Through his mistress's celestial beauty the lover received a moral education, which led his thoughts away from bodily desires. So Spenser tells his lady in Sonnet VIII of the *Amoretti*:

> Through your bright beams doth not the blinded guest*
> Shoot out his darts to base affections wound;
> But angels come to lead frail minds to rest
> In chaste desires, on heavenly beauty bound.

Donne does not entirely reject this neoplatonic conception of love, for in some of the poems which read as though addressed to Ann More—in *The Relic*, for instance—he describes a mistress with whom only spiritual union is possible. In *The Ecstasy*, making a more balanced judgement between the opposing claims of body and spirit in love, he speaks of the lovers' mutual understanding through a union of souls and acknowledges that 'it was not sex' which brought them together; but he also enters a passionate plea for the body to be allowed its part in their union; 'Else a great prince in prison lies'. But in *The Flea*, almost certainly with the intention of scandalizing his readers, he writes as though seduction and physical satisfaction were all that concerned the lover. This downright attitude is accompanied by a matching toughness of mind towards the mistress. He does not appeal for pity, or beg her to save him from heartbroken death by giving up her virginity; but with the peremptory command, 'Mark but this flea', he embarks upon a strenuous intellectual demonstration proving that she has no grounds for resisting him. It is a game he plays to win, and whose outcome is never seriously in doubt. If the poem has any deeper significance beneath Donne's witty outraging of convention, it would seem to lie in the wrestling with ideas by which Donne subdues an opposing argument, and makes himself master of an imaginary situation.

The Sun Rising

> Busy old fool, unruly sun,
>   Why dost thou thus
> Through windows and through curtains call on us?
> Must to thy motions lovers' seasons run?
>   Saucy pedantic wretch, go chide
>   Late schoolboys and sour prentices;
> Go tell court huntsmen that the king will ride;
> Call country ants to harvest offices.
> Love, all alike, no season knows nor clime,
> 10 Nor hours, days, months, which are the rags of time.

*i.e., Cupid

> Thy beams so reverend and strong
>> Why shouldst thou think?
> I could eclipse and cloud them with a wink,
> But that I would not lose her sight so long.
>> If her eyes have not blinded thine,
>>> Look, and tomorrow late tell me
>> Whether both the Indias of spice and mine   [gold]
>> Be where thou left'st them, or lie here with me.
> Ask for those kings whom thou saw'st yesterday,
> 20   And thou shalt hear, all here in one bed lay.
>
>> She is all states, and all princes I,
>>> Nothing else is.
> Princes do but play us; compared to this,
> All honour's mimic, all wealth alchemy.
>> Thou, sun, art half as happy as we
>>> In that the world's contracted thus;
>> Thine age asks ease, and since thy duties be
>> To warm the world, that's done in warming us.
> Shine here to us, and thou art everywhere;
> 30   This bed thy centre is, these walls thy sphere.

The Sun Rising is another poem with a victorious outcome, though here Donne does not set himself the task of outwitting and overcoming his mistress. In point of the poet's relationship with the lady, this poem conforms more closely with Petrarchan convention; though not in making its setting a bedroom where the lovers lie in bed together. Sexual achievement has not disillusioned the poet, for he refers to his mistress with pride and boastful admiration; making hyperbolic claims for her beauty beside which the conventional lover's praises seem modest. The satirical attitude towards woman found in the three previous poems is transformed into the rhapsodic happiness of a lover who knows himself so closely integrated with his mistress that they form their own world:

> She is all states, and all princes I:
> Nothing else is.

Where before the poet's confidence springs from his awareness of his intellectual and rhetorical superiority over the woman, it is now based upon the deeper emotional assurance of love returned. Yet even with this settled assurance, Donne seems unable to abandon his habit of attacking and subduing a force which resists him. So, despite his happiness as a lover in *The Sun Rising*, this poem is not addressed to the mistress but to the sun who has disturbed their enjoyment, and whose busybody behaviour the lover resents as much as his fussy punctuality. The poem begins with an outburst of insulting phrases, 'Busy old fool, unruly sun . . . Saucy pedantic wretch', which directly parallel the terms of abuse applied to the cruel or deceitful mistress in other poems: 'vain lunatic', 'murderess', 'feigned vestal'. As the

E

poem develops we recognize that it has a double purpose; in part to make a triumphant proclamation of the poet's good fortune as a lover, but more perhaps to answer the sun's challenge by rebuking his impudence and petty-minded concern with time, and by correcting his mistaken sense of duty. By the end of the poem Donne seems to have persuaded the sun to adopt his own point of view, and to regard the lovers not merely as the centre-point of the universe, but as the earth itself.

This double purpose gives *The Sun Rising* a special poetic interest, for as the speaker's attention shifts from the sun to his mistress, his tone varies from angry protest and scorn to lazy content; and the emotional texture of the poem thus changes repeatedly. The opening is indignant and irascible; the lover demanding an explanation of the sun's ill-mannered intrusion:

> Busy old fool, unruly sun,
> Why dost thou thus
> Through windows and through curtains call on us?
> Must to thy motions lovers' seasons run?

Then, as though the initial shock of displeasure has been absorbed, the lover opens a second phase of attack consisting of more pointed personal insult, jeering at the humble duties which the sun must perform in the world that is ruled by his movements:

> Saucy pedantic wretch, go chide
> Late schoolboys and sour prentices;
> Go tell court huntsmen that the king will ride;
> Call country ants to harvest offices.

In this last line the pace of the poem, so angrily impetuous a little before, has slackened perceptibly, as though to represent the sluggishness of harvesters turning out of bed. Their sleepy reluctance brings the lover back to his own deep comfort of mind and body; and as he contemplates his shared happiness the lines stretch out and become almost immobilized by the weight of stressed syllables, their movement checked like the flow of time within the lovers' room:

> Love, all alike, no season knows, nor clime,
> Nor hours, days, months, which are the rags of time.

The language is commonplace, almost drab; it includes no images and no explicit reference to feeling, and yet the whole statement is richly sensuous in its suggestion of relaxed and contented wellbeing. It is a mark of Donne's poetic strength that without inviting help from figurative or romantic terms he can make such worn colloquial language carry a potent emotional charge. His secret lies in the close matching of verse rhythms to the current of feeling which underlies the speaker's words, so that the reader seems to hear his emotional experience as the verse picks its way forward, now checked and now with a rush of eloquence. After the suggested luxury and ease of lines

9 and 10, the second stanza opens with another burst of scornful arrogance:

> Thy beams so reverend and strong
> Why shouldst thou think?

By stressing all four syllables of the short line, Donne gives the question a ring of personal assurance which makes what follows—the lover's boast that he could himself eclipse the sun, if he were willing to lose sight of his mistress for a moment—seem more than conceited swagger. When he goes on to the hyperbolic challenge of the next four lines, we are consequently not disposed to ridicule his suggestion; for we have been made to sense the deep emotional conviction which it represents. The experience of such absolute love can only be conveyed in subjective terms, and however exaggerated the idea itself, the measured emphasis of Donne's statement makes us feel—or again, hear—his unshakeable assurance:

> If her eyes have not blinded thine,
> Look, and tomorrow late, tell me
> Whether both the Indias of spice and mine
> Be where thou left'st them, or lie here with me.

As in the first stanza, he has now lost the angry impatience of his rebuke to the sun, and is again relaxing into the warm emotional serenity which makes his grand assertions seem like calm statements of fact:

> Ask for those kings whom thou saw'st yesterday,
> And thou shalt hear, all here in one bed lay.

By loading the last phrase—of its six monosyllabic words, only one is unstressed—Donne again creates an impression of solid conviction and truth. If the poet's remark seemed excited and impulsive, we should see its hyperbole as a lover's exaggeration and laugh at his romantic idea. In fact, it sounds like a soberly considered judgment, expressed in the plainest and most unpretentious language. Drawing upon no sensuous terms, and making 'kings' supply all the imaginative suggestions of splendour which he requires, Donne evokes a sense of fulfilment so complete that nothing less than the simplest form of words can represent it.

The idea of 'those kings' leads to the opening statement of the third stanza, in which the lover's hyperbole goes beyond all its previous limits of daring.

> She is all states, and all princes I;
> Nothing else is.

Again the weight and sober pace of the remark help to transform what might be an extravagant boast into a simple, entirely credible declaration. The lover's claim that, apart from themselves, nothing exists—'Nothing else is'—reduces hyperbole to the level of plain fact by words so stark and basic that no other sense can be read into them. We might expect a lover so ecstatically happy to make himself a little ridiculous by overpraising his mistress's beauty or by swearing eternal constancy, but Donne ignores these familiar gambits of love poetry. He describes his mistress in geographical terms, 'both the Indias of spice and mine', 'all states', and not by comparing her with precious stones and mythological figures; and he represents his rapture directly, as though by allowing the reader to take his pulse, and not by painting the lady's portrait. A lover might be mistaken in his judgment of the mistress's beauty, but the experience which he undergoes as he contemplates her cannot be either true or false; and it is this actuality of sensation which Donne sets himself to represent. The statement that 'princes do but play us' has no validity outside the poem, but it is not offered as a view of objective fact: it represents the sense of sovereignty and vital importance which springs from the lover's assured knowledge of his shared happiness. The terms 'mimic' and 'alchemy' applied to other kinds of distinction imply that they are worthless in comparison. This claims a good deal less than the opening remark of the same stanza, and yet is unconvincing; probably because the comparison implies that the lover is no longer absorbed in his personal situation, but looking beyond it.

If this is a weakness, the poem immediately recovers. The last four lines consist of a metaphysical argument—more exactly, of a proof by sophistry—showing that by shining upon the lovers the sun will be carrying out its appointed duty:

Shine here to us, and thou art everywhere:
This bed thy centre is, these walls thy sphere.*

The emphatic tone of the statement, and the uncompromising bareness of its language, reaffirm the speaker's absolute assurance; not merely as a lover but as an aggressive individualist who has challenged a greater force, and by sheer energy and determination bent him to his will. However successful as a love poem, *The Sun Rising* takes its dynamism from the poet's conflict with an authority whom he refuses to acknowledge, and who is forced to accept the poet's mastery. The sense of angry conflict is deeply alien to the lyrical mood which had seemed most natural to love poetry hitherto; but Donne seems to have found conflict an essential condition of his imaginative activity.

*In the context of Elizabethan astronomy, the term 'centre' signifies the earth, which stands at the centre of the universe. 'Sphere' has roughly the same sense as 'orbit' in modern English. Donne is thinking like a Ptolemaic astronomer, and not like a Copernican.

The Relic

When my grave is broke up again,
Some second guest to entertain—
For graves have learnt that womanhead,
To be to more than one a bed—
     And he that digs it spies
(A bracelet of bright hair about the bone,)
     Will he not let's alone,
And think that there a loving couple lies,
Who thought that this device might be some way
10 To make their souls, at the last busy day,
Meet at this grave and make a little stay?

If this fall in a time or land
Where misdevotion doth command,
Then he that digs us up will bring
Us to the bishop and the king,
     To make us relics: then
Thou shalt be a Mary Magdalen, and I
     A something else thereby.
All women shall adore us, and some men;
20 And since at such time miracles are sought,
I would have that age by this paper taught
What miracles we harmless lovers wrought.

First, we loved well and faithfully,
Yet knew not what we loved, nor why;
Difference of sex no more we knew
Than our guardian angels do:
     Coming and going, we
Perchance might kiss, but not between those meals:
     Our hands ne'er touched the seals
30 Which nature, injured by late law, sets free.
These miracles we did; but now, alas,
All measure and all language I should pass,
Should I tell what a miracle she was.

This characteristic of his writing is less evident in *The Relic*, which like *The Sun Rising* is addressed to his partner in a true love-match. It is much unlike the previous poem in its sombre subject matter, for here Donne contemplates a point of time after his death, when his grave will be opened and his bones thrown out to make room for another occupant. If *The Sun Rising* was strikingly unconventional, at least the lovers' situation was realistically appropriate; but the opening words of *The Relic*,

When my grave is broke up again,
Some second guest to entertain,

seem to have no conceivable application to a love poem. By making such an idea his starting-point, Donne shows how unpredictably his mind works; here finding a path from the macabre idea of being disinterred to the notion of holy relics, and then to an account of his loving relationship with his mistress. But the conceit which brings these ideas together is unforced, and the whole poem represents a steady and persistent growth of thought from the unexpected opening concept to the rueful admission with which it ends. Although the associations of idea are odd in themselves, within the working-out of Donne's curiously involved argument they are seen to happen naturally and spontaneously. The complete poem allows us to trace the form of an elaborate mental experience as it occurred—or rather, as it was thought into being—within Donne's creative consciousness.

Unlike the other poems we have considered, *The Relic* opens quietly. When his grave is reopened, Donne says, and the gravedigger comes across a bone encircled with a bracelet of his mistress' hair,* perhaps he will suppose that 'a loving couple' lie there, hoping to be reunited on Judgment Day, and will leave them undisturbed. If this should happen during a period of 'misdevotion' or false religion, the gravedigger will carry these relics to the bishop, to be venerated as holy things: her hair as though it had belonged to another Mary Magdalen, the bone as though it came from one of her lovers. Together they will be adored; and as miracles will be expected of them, this poem sets down for future ages what wonderful things they have already performed. The great miracle lay in the virtuousness of their behaviour as lovers whose relationship ignored sex, who kissed only at meeting and parting, and who never challenged the moral law which restrains natural impulse. This miracle he can describe, but to give any proper account of her miraculous self lies beyond the power of poetry. Presumably the poet speaks of his mistress in the past tense here because he is imagining a time when she will be long dead, and not because he has already lost her. The tone of regret in this final statement helps to subdue the speaker's feelings, and to maintain the unusual reserve which Donne imposes upon his volatile temperament throughout this almost wistful poem.

Despite its macabre opening theme, *The Relic* has some flashes of comic wit which show Donne's readiness to joke even when his subject is generally serious. The notion of his grave being emptied, 'some second guest to entertain', is expressed in wrily ironic terms, and without any of the horror or indignation which such a prospect might arouse. There follows a remark about graves learning from women how 'to be to more than one a bed', which although not very complimentary to the mistress, proves that Donne's mood is less sombre than his subject. This playful spirit continues as he suggests that the gravedigger may think the relic a device contrived by the lovers to ensure a meeting on Judgment Day: as the resurrected souls reassume

*For a second poem on this love-token, 'that subtle wreath of hair which crowns my arm', see *The Funeral*.

their bodies, the mistress must come to the lover's grave to claim the lock of hair woven into the bracelet. The idea itself is comic in its ingenuity, and becomes more amusing when Donne suggests that the gravedigger may hit on this explanation of the relic. There is another touch of levity in the reference to Judgment Day, where 'busy' seems to imply a homely occasion, such as a market-day, with no awesome solemnity but a good deal of haste and agitation.

In the second stanza Donne's humour takes a sly and possibly daring turn. When the relics have been accepted by the Church—not, of course, the Anglican faith, which did not admit them—then, Donne supposes,

> Thou shalt be a Mary Magdalen, and I
> A something else thereby.

This does not flatter the mistress, for before her conversion Mary Magdalen was a prostitute; but perhaps Donne would answer her protest by arguing that the mistake proved the blindness of the 'misdevotion' which he leaves us to identify. The comment about himself, who will be judged 'a something else thereby'—that is, through his association with Mary Magdalen—is mischievously comic. He may mean that he will be regarded as one of her customers, redeemed by his association with the saint whom she became: a reading encouraged by the reluctant pause after 'I', where the line-unit breaks the sentence. Alternatively, Donne may be hinting that his bone will be venerated as a relic of Christ, 'thereby' alluding to this more decorous aspect of the Magdalen's life. If this suggestion seems profane, Donne is still protected by the terms of his story; for it is not he but the idolatrous worshippers who will make the assumption. Whichever reading we prefer, Donne is bringing his comic wit to bear upon himself. It may be merely a private impression that the tone of 'a something else' is rueful, and that the speaker's unwillingness to be explicit is explained by the ignominious name to be put upon him. The line which follows, 'All women shall adore us, and some men', appears to support this reading. Donne is still showing some playful disrespect for woman in her romantic credulity: man is generally above such folly, though 'some men' admits that his sex too may succumb. The possibility that he will be mistaken for one of the Magdalen's clients is more in keeping with this ironically disparaging manner than with a profane suggestion that he will be mistaken for Christ.*

In the third stanza Donne drops his playful mood and speaks altogether seriously. He has been prepared to joke about the disturbance of his grave and the preposterous likelihood of becoming a holy relic; but when he begins to describe the virtuous love between himself and his mistress the tone of the poem changes. Where previously he has been definite and factual, even though writing about future events, he now admits uncertainty and vagueness: as lovers (lines 23, 24),

---

* One might add that the slur implicit in 'some men' seems to be aimed at woman's romantic disposition to sentimentalize over a lover, and not at man's tendency to agnosticism.

> we loved well and faithfully,
> Yet knew not what we loved, nor why.

The main sense of this remark is repeated in the next two lines (25, 26), which in idiom and idea suggest the innocence and simplicity of children:

> Difference of sex no more we knew
> Than our guardian angels do.

The image is doubly appropriate: angels are sexless, and the simile suggests their watchful presence protecting the lovers against sin. These are not the 'strong lines' of metaphysical writing, but in their quietness an evocation of almost tender feeling. Donne has changed his viewpoint, no longer predicting the future as a mocking realist but looking back—seemingly over a long span of time —to the period of this miraculous love, when his mistress was still alive. As we see from the legal image of breaking a seal in line 29, he makes no outward concession to romantic feeling, but follows his habitual practice of describing passionate experience—here, making love—in intellectual terms. None the less, the last stanza leaves an impression of wistfulness and nostalgia that is difficult to reconcile with its characteristically plain language and analytic detachment. This impression seems to derive chiefly from the changed manner of the last stanza. After the levity and fantastic wit of the two opening stanzas, Donne reaches the inner subject of the poem; and in his change of voice we recognize the deep emotion which has allowed him to play with ideas of gravedigging and the Last Judgment in so light-hearted a spirit.

The five poems so far considered are all markedly individual in form. *The Flea* has three nine-line stanzas, rhyming in couplets for six lines and concluding in a triple rhyme. *Woman's Constancy* has a more complicated structure. Its seventeen lines vary in length between five and two feet, and do not make a symmetrical pattern; and its rhyme scheme is no less complex. Lines 1–4 and 12–17 rhyme in couplets, but the seven lines which make up the middle of the poem present a problem which Donne solves by rhyming *cccdeed*; so that altogether its form is unpredictable. *The Sun Rising* consists of three ten-line stanzas, but the rhythm which they impose upon the poem is again a complicated one. The rhyme scheme is part of this complexity, *abba*, *cdcd*, *ee*, varying throughout the stanza as do the line-units, whose length fluctuates from two to five feet. These three examples characterize Donne's ingenuity in contriving the stanza form that will both contain his ideas and become part of their sense. The shape of each poem is, as it were, tailormade to suit the experience which Donne represents, and could not be used for any other purpose. But the *Valediction forbidding Mourning* is atypical of Donne's practice. It is set in the simplest of quatrains, with lines of even length rhyming alternately; and at first sight does not look like a metaphysical poem at all. However, Donne has chosen this unpretentious form with a purpose.

A Valediction forbidding Mourning

As virtuous men pass mildly away,
   And whisper to their souls to go,
Whilst some of their sad friends do say
    The breath goes now, and some say no;

So let us melt and make no noise,
   No tear-floods nor sigh-tempests move;
T'were profanation of our joys
    To tell the laity our love.

Moving of th'earth brings harms and fears,
10   Men reckon what it did and meant;
But trepidation of the spheres,
    Though greater far, is innocent.

Dull sublunary lovers' love,
   Whose soul is sense, cannot admit
Absence, because it doth remove
    Those things which elemented it.

But we, by a love so much refined
   That ourselves know not what it is,
Interassured of the mind,
20   Care less eyes, lips and hands to miss.

Our two souls, therefore, which are one,
   Though I must go, endure not yet
A breach, but an expansion,
    Like gold to airy thinness beat.

If they be two, they are two so
   As stiff twin compasses are two;
Thy soul, the fixed foot, makes no show
    To move, but doth if th'other do:

And though it in the centre sit,
30   Yet when the other far doth roam
It leans and hearkens after it,
    And grows erect as that comes home.

Such wilt thou be to me, who must
   Like the other foot, obliquely run;
Thy firmness makes my circle just,
    And makes me end where I begun.

This *Valediction* is one of several poems addressed to a woman by a lover about to leave on a journey or voyage which must separate them for some considerable while. Whether any of them were written for Donne's wife does not immediately concern us, for they would not be intrinsically better poems simply because that were so. Most readers would agree that, whatever the circumstances, this poem is one of the finest of the *Songs and Sonets*, for despite its out-of-the-way allusions and images, a sense of firm and deeply-based emotion is evoked from the first and consistently maintained. T. S. Eliot's phrase about the 'direct sensuous apprehension of thought' would be misapplied here, for it is rather feeling which is given expression through intellectual concepts. The central concern of this poem is to define the relationship between the lovers which makes separation unimportant, or even impossible; and to this end Donne works out equivalents for the force which binds and unifies the lovers, drawing analogies from the impersonal field of science and craftsmanship.

The poem begins with an analogy which, although 'metaphysical' in its witty incongruity, includes a striking and entirely successful image of sensation. Their parting, the speaker is telling his mistress, must not involve a show of extravagant grief but a silent melting from one another; and as illustration he suggests a death so imperceptible that the watchers at the bedside cannot tell when the last breath is taken:

> Whilst some of their sad friends do say
> The breath goes now, and some say no.

The alliterated s-sounds in the first line make us hear the whispering about the dying man, and the assonance which links 'now . . . no' in the next line continues this sound effect, by representing the faint respiration which the friends are straining to hear. Thus while at first sight the analogy seems either strained or hackneyed—separation is death for all true lovers—its ideas are realized with such immediacy and conviction that we must accept it. However unlikely a parallel in its broad form, it contains an image of untroubled separation so apt that its incongruous details drop out of sight. In such passages the oddities of metaphysical style justify themselves completely in their imaginative effect.

In its inhibition of emotional display, this work is pointedly unlike another of Donne's valedictory poems, *Of Weeping*, where the lovers' tears and sighs become the subject of elaborate conceits designed to exhibit the speaker's ingenuity as much as his grief. In *A Valediction forbidding Mourning* Donne does not merely urge the lady to be reticent, but shows restraint himself by adopting a simple poetic form and a manner which invites none of his characteristic flamboyance. When he tells his mistress that it would profane their happiness 'to tell the laity our love'—meaning those who have not been admitted to its holy mysteries—we believe him, although the poem does broadcast the fact; for its tone is consistent with a wish to avoid making a show of private feeling. Their grief, Donne argues, is in any case too profound to be expressed by such means: earthquakes cause terror and perplexity, but the much greater movement of the spheres brought about by trepidation* is regarded as a natural occurrence, and upsets

---

*An oscillating movement of the heavens, which makes the planets appear to go backwards—that is, from east to west—over part of their orbit. Its actual cause is a slight wobble in the earth's axis.

no one. The scientific parallel suggests that their parting, though far more momentous than any ordinary separation, must attract much less attention. Lovers of a 'dull sublunary' kind, Donne argues, know nothing beyond physical love; and cannot reconcile themselves to parting because, for them, bodily separation is absolute. All sublunary beings are subject to change and decay, and in applying this term to other lovers Donne implies that he and she have the constancy and permanence found above the moon. For them, whose love has been purified to such a degree that they themselves cannot comprehend it, loss of physical contact is much less important. The phrase, 'interassured of the mind', seems openly to admit the need for unshakeable security which Donne so often represents, as much in the argumentative structure of his poems as in the passionate insistence of its working-out. The lovers form a single being, sharing a single soul; and their unity is not to be fractured by physical separation. Rather, their shared soul will extend itself as the gap between their bodies widens, 'Like gold to airy thinness beat' (line 24).

This delicate and richly suggestive analogy deserves closer attention than the more famous image of compasses which follows. In drawing a link between ideas as disparate as lovers' relationships and the goldsmith's craft, Donne makes a typically unexpected proposal, and again justifies himself imaginatively. Other metals—copper and lead, for instance—can be beaten into sheets, but none of them so impalpably thin as gold leaf; nor do other metals have the beauty, value and noble associations of gold. Donne's image gives the lovers' shared soul these splendid qualities, yet at the same time suggests its insubstantial nature through the evocative phrase 'airy thinness'. No other literary mode, one feels, could have enabled a poet to describe spiritual being in terms so concrete and yet so closely sympathetic to his argument.

Wisely perhaps, Donne does not develop this fine image, but shifts his ground to a further comparison which provides the theme of the three final stanzas. If the lovers do not share a common soul, Donne argues, then their individual souls are firmly joined together, like the legs of a pair of compasses: meaning the instrument which we now call dividers. Probably no other image is used so often to illustrate metaphysical poetry, and it might be well to point out that Donne has other interests than mathematics and navigation, and that his compasses do not necessarily involve a reference to some new science. What is more typical of metaphysical style is the way Donne extends and develops his initial idea, by arguing a series of parallels between the spiritually linked lovers and the joined legs of the compasses. 'Thy soul, the fixed foot' (line 27), he tells his partner, is not impelled to move until he does so, but then follows his example. In the same way, when the outer leg of the dividers describes a circle, its partner marking the centre turns about, as though watching. Again, when the outer leg describes an arc at the limit of its reach, its partner 'leans and hearkens after it' as though straining to keep in contact; and draws itself up straight when the outer leg completes its circular journey and 'comes home'. This corresponds with their own relationship, Donne tells the lady. Like the leg which describes the circle, he must trace out his traveller's course while she, the fixed foot, remains in one place.

His comment (line 34) 'Thy firmness makes my circle just,' is not easily paraphrased. The moving leg of the compasses describes a true circle only because the other holds its position throughout. This fixity represents the constancy and fidelity of the woman, and the assurance of her 'firmness' gives Donne the power to make his own circle true: both loving her with equal constancy, and throughout his journey moving along a line that must bring him back to his starting-point in her. The analogy is not exact, for when the outer leg of the compasses completes its circle it is at the same distance from the centre as during its movement; and obviously Donne means the closing of the circle to represent reunion at the end of the journey. This true circle has been drawn by their combined strengths, and its symbol of perfection stands for their flawless relationship and—perhaps not accidentally—for the rounded achievement of this poem.

Holy Sonnet XIV

Batter my heart, three-personed God, for you
As yet but knock, breathe, shine and seek to mend;
That I may rise and stand, o'erthrow me and bend
Your force to break, blow, burn and make me new.
I, like an usurped town to another due,
Labour to admit you, but O to no end:
Reason, your viceroy in me, me should defend,
But is captived, and proves weak or untrue.
Yet dearly I love you, and would be loved fain,
10   But am betrothed unto your enemy:
Divorce me, untie or break that knot again;
Take me to you, imprison me, for I
Except you enthral me, never shall be free,
Nor ever chaste, except you ravish me.

The *Songs and Sonets* were written when Donne was a young man, and probably during the years immediately before and after his marriage in 1601. The nineteen *Holy Sonnets* belong to a later and darker period of his life, when the death of his wife in 1617 robbed him of his greatest comfort, and profoundly changed his personal outlook. These poems reflect a deep disturbance of spirit, and suggest that with his wife's death Donne lost the vital sense of security to which many of his love poems refer. He now looks to God for an assurance of love, but haunted by the recollection of his sins Donne seems unable to persuade himself either that he deserves or that he can expect divine forgiveness. His spiritual anxiety, sometimes rising to a climax of terror, as when he contemplates the possible imminence of God's judgment, 'What if this present were the world's last night?' (*XIII.* 1) is felt in the choked utterance of these poems, which wrench language and metre into strained phrases, to represent Donne's agitation directly.

The element of dialectic found in the love poems reappears in these sonnets, sharpened and given muscle by a more urgent need to prove—whether to himself or to God—that he can be saved from damnation. We may be incongruously reminded of the younger Donne's use of dialectic to silence a woman's resistance, or to justify inconstancy; for although the matter of the *Holy Sonnets* is utterly different, the poet's arguments are still forced to their conclusion without respect for a logical progression of ideas. Despite appearances they, like the love poems, are motivated by passionate impulse; and whether the argument hangs together matters much less than whether the poem resolves the alarm or disquiet which triggers Donne's attempt to reason himself into a state of spiritual calm.

The emotional explosiveness of the *Holy Sonnets* is countered by their structural formality. They have the usual fourteen lines of the Elizabethan sonnet, each of five feet; and they observe the usual division into octet and sestet. Their rhyme scheme is less familiar. Instead of rhyming in quatrains, *abab*, *cdcd*, Donne completes the octet with only two rhymes, which fall irregularly: *abba*, *abba*. This helps to unify the octet, but calls for a stricter discipline in shaping expression; and this demand upon the poet's craftsmanship acts as a brake on the vehement feeling which impels his poem. In *Sonnet XIV* this driving force manifests itself in an opening sentence as brutally violent as the treatment it appeals for:

Batter my heart, three-personed God; for you
As yet but knock, breathe, shine, and seek to mend.

The suddenness of the onslaught takes us unawares, and the strongly accented verbs 'knock, breathe, shine' ring like hammer-blows: fittingly, for Donne is making the lines act out the furious bombardment which will break his enslavement to sin and make him God's captive. He longs to be rescued from his sinfulness, but knows himself so hopelessly subjugated that gentle inducements cannot persuade him to reform; and he cries out to be overwhelmed by the power of God, which will shatter and then re-create him:

That I may rise and stand, o'erthrow me and bend
Your force to break, blow, burn and make me new.

After the check on 'stand' the voice leaps forward, telescoping the phrase 'o'erthrow me and bend' into a rush of sound; but in the next line the movement is again halted, and three more fiercely stressed words, 'break, blow, burn' hack into an almost obliterated metrical pattern. Within less than two lines, Donne has passed from rushing haste to something near immobility, first breaking down the natural stops in verse rhythm, and then setting harshly unnatural barriers across it. Altogether seven passages of this sonnet are elided, where Donne crushes words together to make them fit the decasyllabic line.* Nominally, he respects this verse form; for however he wrenches and compresses language, the line does not run to more than five feet; but as he rams words into blurred phrases, or dislocates the line unit with fiercely stressed monosyllables, Donne seems to be straining sonnet form to the point of breakdown. The impression that the lines can barely contain all that he crams into them is chiefly responsible for the explosive effect of this poem: through it we feel the speaker's desperation as he seeks to move God to take sterner measures with him.

The sense of violence is greatest in the opening four lines; a fact partly explained by the remarkable number of verbs which they include. The next four lines involve a change of tone, as Donne drops from the imperative to the apologetic and explains to God how powerless he is to resist sin unaided:

> I, like an usurped town to another due,
> Labour to admit you, but O to no end:
> Reason, your viceroy in me, me should defend,
> But is captived, and proves weak or untrue.

The suggestion of an armed conflict in Donne's simile might seen inappropriate to a man's relationship with God, but in the context of violent physical effort established by the opening lines of the sonnet, ideas of siege and warfare follow as though naturally. We might expect prayer to be respectful and submissive, but Donne shows as little regard for custom in his devotional writing as in his love poetry; and his image of a conquered city feebly trying to readmit its dis-possessed prince seizes upon the reality of his spiritual state, ignoring polite convention. As a lover he disregards the usual forms of com-pliment, not troubling to describe his mistress's features but con-centrating upon the vital subject of what unites her to him. In much the same way when he addresses God he goes straight to the crucial point, not attempting to praise God or to offer humble service but demanding to be told God's purposes towards him, or clamouring to be assured that he can be admitted to God's grace. The sonnet *Batter my heart* is typically of this aggressive and insistent approach, and of Donne's honesty in the moral self-appraisal which lies immediately behind his appeal. His innate inclination to sin is too strong a force to be reversed by his puny moral impulse; yet as he explains to God, he longs to be united with him. The voice which at the beginning of the poem is fiercely demanding now becomes muted and wistful:

---

*The seven phrases are, 'me and bend', 'to another', 'to admit', 'dearly love', 'you and', 'me, untie', and 'you enthral'. In each of them two syllables are run together to form a single sound. Some editors indicate elision in Donne typographically, for instance, 't'another', 't'admit', and 'dearly'I love'.

Yet dearly I love you, and would be loved fain,
But am betrothed unto your enemy.

The idiom of the poem has changed radically, and so has Donne's metaphor. His relationship with God, seen in terms of physical conflict previously, is now presented as the unsatisfied yearning of a lover; and although this is a more familiar concept, Donne exploits his analogy with a particularity which transforms it. No longer in the thick of a spiritual battle, he speaks as a woman forced into a marriage contract against her will, who looks despairingly towards the man she loves, hoping that he may still claim her. This development of Donne's original idea seems to dislocate the poem by its unexpectedness, but in the closing four lines he brings the images of physical violence and passionate love together, as he renews his tormented appeal to be overwhelmed by God:

Divorce me, untie or break that knot again;
Take me to you, imprison me; for I
Unless you enthrall me, never shall be free,
Nor ever chaste except you ravish me.

The image of sexual violation might be thought grotesquely inappropriate to the relationship of God and man. But what we know of Donne's temperament through his style tells us how turbulent his feelings were, and we recognize that this startling analogy reflects a mode of apprehension natural to him, and not a deliberate attempt to be sensational. If he is to feel secure, God must take him with the sudden ferocity of possession which the metaphor implies; and thus although the image may be theologically doubtful, in terms of feeling it is amply justified. Moreover, by combining the concepts of love and violence which provide the poem's two main imaginative themes, the metaphor of rape ties together these diverse elements of Donne's argument in a firmly unified conclusion.

Despite the power of Donne's images in this sonnet, not they but his argument dominates the poem. As in several of the love poems, here too Donne's emotional energy is harnessed to an intellectual task; and by the end of the sonnet he has worked out an answer to his distracting spiritual problem, which he storms at God to accept. Significantly, his answer involves a double paradox: Donne can never be free until God has taken him prisoner, nor chaste until God has possessed him by force. These vary the form of a similar paradox earlier in the poem (line 3), 'That I may rise and stand, o'erthrow me', and together show how much of the poem is directed by intellectual wit. The intensely purposeful argument determines how the sonnet develops, and makes all other features of the poem subordinate to its driving needs. It is this feature of Donne's devotional poetry which distinguishes him most clearly from those who wrote in the later metaphysical manner. His poetry is essentially argument: a hard, stubbornly persistent core of dialectic whose purposes dictate the poem's general form and the particular nature of its images.

George Herbert

Conscience

Peace, prattler, do not lour:
Not a fair look but thou dost call it foul,
Not a sweet dish but thou dost call it sour;
    Music to thee doth howl.
  By list'ning to thy chatting fears
  I have both lost mine eyes and ears.

  Prattler, no more, I say:
My thoughts must work but like a noiseless sphere,
Harmonious peace must rock them all the day;
10   No room for prattlers there.
  If thou persistest, I will tell thee
  That I have physic to expel thee.

  And the receipt shall be
My Saviour's blood: whenever at his board
I do but taste it, straight it cleanseth me,
    And leaves thee not a word;
  No, not a tooth or nail to scratch,
  And at my actions carp or catch.

  Yet if thou talkest still,
20 Besides my physic, know there's some for thee:
Some wood and nails to make a staff or bill
    For those that trouble me.
  The bloody cross of my dear Lord
  Is both my physic and my sword.

This quality is much less apparent in the work of his closest successor, Herbert. In place of Donne's driving intellectual energy, Herbert contrives an unhurried and usually well-mannered exposition in which an element of picturesque charm frequently plays an important part. Where Donne's language is usually tough and abrasive, Herbert's has a gentle grace; and his characteristic fondness for simple proverbial terms and colloquial expressions softens any tendency in his work towards the intellectual aggressiveness of Donne. The opening lines of *Conscience* typify the note of homely simplicity which Herbert so often evokes:

  Peace, prattler, do not lour:
Not a fair look but thou dost call it foul;
Not a sweet dish but thou dost call it sour.

Although the poet is addressing his conscience, the familiar terms of his rebuke suggest that its subject is much less consequential. Herbert talks down to his conscience, as though it were a bothersome child whose grumbling had tried his patience long enough. The disturbance is on a very small scale, and a sharp warning will be enough to bring the troublemaker to his senses. Where Donne leaves the impression of a man racked by spiritual conflict, unable to silence or even to modify the terror which his conscience raises, Herbert easily puts aside the worrying voice which interrupts his inward calm (lines 7–10):

> Prattler, no more, I say:
> My thoughts must work but like a noiseless sphere,
> Harmonious peace must rock them all the day:
> No room for prattlers there.

The first and second stanzas open with much the same remark. There is no progression of idea, but a restatement of the same attitude; and although this at once establishes the rhythmical pulse of the poem, it denies Herbert the driving force which impels Donne's argument. Such a sense of intellectual energy thrusting a path through obstacles and doubts was clearly not to Herbert's purpose. His writing betrays a fondness for the diminutive and the picturesque, and he frequently presents himself in these terms; a quiet and gentle-mannered figure whose spiritual crises barely ruffle the surface of his simple faith. Unlike Donne, he has no need to batter at the locked door of divine mercy, or to twist ideas into irrefutable proof of his personal salvation. The motive of Donne's metaphysical argument is missing, and Herbert is free to devote himself to the quaint and outlandish ideas which, in Donne, had been offshoots of this central dialectic. The images of the final stanza of *Conscience* are typical of Herbert's manner. When he speaks of 'some wood and nails' he is referring to the Cross, but in such a homely and familiar way that we might mistake his purpose:

> Yet if thou talkest still,
> Besides my physic, know there's some for thee:
> Some wood and nails to make a staff or bill
> For those that trouble me.
> The bloody cross of my dear Lord
> Is both my physic and my sword.

His manner of referring to the materials of the Cross takes away their special religious associations, and makes them seem no more significant than the lath and tintacks of a toy sword. Herbert habitually reduces the scale of figures and events in this way. So far as this makes the central ideas of his faith more accessible, he may be justified in bringing them down to an everyday level; but perhaps Herbert is more attracted by the charm of littleness. For him there are no grand and terrible conflicts, and his poetry is predominantly lyrical. Whatever he learnt from Donne, he was much closer in feeling and outlook to the writer of the twenty-third Psalm.

Henry Vaughan

Corruption

Sure, it was so. Man in those early days
  Was not all stone and earth;
He shined a little, and by those weak rays
  Had some glimpse of his birth.
He saw heaven o'er his head, and knew from whence
  He came, condemned, hither;
And, as first love draws strongest, so from hence
  His mind sure progressed thither.
Things here were strange unto him: sweat, and till,
10   All was a thorn or weed;
Nor did those last, but—like himself—died still
  As soon as they did seed.
They seemed to quarrel with him; for that act
  That fell him, foiled them all:
He drew the curse upon the world, and cracked
  The whole frame with his fall.
This made him long for home, as loth to stay
  With murmurers and foes;
He sighed for Eden, and would often say,
20   'Ah, what bright days were those!'
Nor was heaven cold unto him, for each day
  The valley or the mountain
Afforded visits, and still Paradise lay
  In some green shade or fountain.
Angels lay lieger here: each bush and cell,   [resident]
  Each oak and highway knew them;
Walk but the fields, or sit down at some well,
  And he was sure to view them.
Almighty Love, where art thou now? Mad man
30   Sits down and freezeth on;
He raves, and swears to stir nor fire nor fan,
  But bids the thread be spun.
I see thy curtains are close-drawn; thy bow
  Looks dim too in the cloud;
Sin triumphs still, and man is sunk below
  The centre, and his shroud:
All's in deep sleep and night, thick darkness lies
  And hatcheth o'er thy people;
But hark, what trumpet's that? What angel cries,
40   'Arise: thrust in thy sickle!'

Vaughan, here represented by the poem *Corruption*, differs from Herbert in the generally sombre tone of his writing and in his less mannered style. Courtly sensibility plays no part in his poetry, whose colloquial terms have little of Herbert's delicacy and polish. The rougher tone of Vaughan has more immediate kinship with Donne, who is recalled in the abrupt opening phrase of this poem, 'Sure, it was so'; but Donne's dynamic energy and compression will not be found in Vaughan. His poetry does not need these qualities. Where Donne seems to have been straining to realize the actuality of his experience, Vaughan is habitually concerned to indicate the form of a mystic reality behind the appearance of the visible world. In *Corruption* this ultimate reality is at two removes from the reader. Initially, the poem takes us back to Adam after the Expulsion, and to the time when man could still remember 'from whence he came' and the happiness of his first innocence. The reader then shares Adam's nostalgic recollections of the state which he has lost, as he sweats and tills among the thorns of the world to which he is condemned as an outcast. This backward look towards lost happiness and simplicity has the same kind of importance for Vaughan as it would acquire for Wordsworth, with the difference that Vaughan is concerned not with childhood but with the state of spiritual perfection which man still glimpses, in himself and the natural world, where 'shadows of eternity'* sometimes remind the soul of its first home. This kind of apprehension could not be expressed through Donne's striking immediacy of language, or by the kind of persistent argument as he often uses.

There is however a structure in this poem by which it acquires a recognizably metaphysical character. Its argument falls into three sections. 'Sure, it was so' opens Vaughan's description of the life which, he insists, Adam and his immediate descendants led in the early days of man's existence outside the Garden, when though fallen he still enjoyed some contact with the heavenly beings who had been his companions (lines 23–6):

> still Paradise lay
> In some green shade or fountain.
> Angels lay lieger here: each bush and cell,
> Each oak and highway knew them.

By this point the sense of pain and conflict induced by lines 9–16 has been left behind, and Vaughan seems to have settled into a happy contemplation of man's good fortune in the first youth of the world, in surroundings—valley, green shade, fountain—which suggest a pastoral eclogue. But at line 29 he suddenly starts out of this acquiescent mood, as though abruptly recalled to the fact of man's moral corruption which is the tacit starting-point of the poem. The quiet is shattered by an exclamation as forceful as his initial remark:

*The Retreat, l. 14.

> Almighty love, where art thou now? mad man
>   Sits down, and freezeth on.

A mood of despairing protest, centred upon the idea that 'sin triumphs still', replaces completely the poet's previously relaxed frame of mind; and this sombre note deepens almost to the last lines of the poem, where

>   thick darkness lies
> And hatcheth o'er thy people.

The verb 'hatch' has here the sense of brooding, but as though Vaughan also intended it to signify the breaking-out of new life, the line introduces the last of the three startlingly sudden remarks which indicate the poem's main structure:

> But hark, what trumpet's that? What angel cries,
>   'Arise, thrust in thy sickle!'

On this clarion call to arms the poem ends as abruptly as it has begun, dispelling the sense of spiritual depression in a rush of renewed energy and excitement. The three moods of the poem do not merge gradually into one another, and Vaughan does not prepare us for the marked changes of emotional temper. Their suddenness gives the poem its dramatic force and the sense of actual happening that are strongly characteristic of metaphysical writing. We are not allowed to foresee how the poem will develop, and its movements take us as much by surprise as events in real life. Although Vaughan's idiom is generally much less dramatic than Donne's, this jerky development, as we can see from the three separate movements of *The Flea*, is very suggestive of the older poet's style.

In other respects Vaughan shows how diluted the metaphysical element of seventeenth-century poetry had become by 1650 or so. He continues to use the direct conversational manner which Donne had introduced, but the language which Donne uses so vigorously has now lost much of its drive, and seems in danger of lapsing into a chatty casualness. There are still patches of terseness and vernacular colour as in lines 9–10:

> Things here were strange unto him: sweat and till,
>   All was a thorn or weed;

but there are some flat and nerveless lines which lack the intellectual drive we may expect of metaphysical poetry:

> Walk but the fields, or sit down at some well,
>   And he was sure to view them.

The statement is too limp to communicate a sense of sureness, and Vaughan seems trying only to be agreeable. The poem is written without the pressure of intellectual engagement that is so marked in Donne, and in consequence the element of verbal wit contributes very little to the poem. Vaughan introduces two conceits; a comparison between man and the plants, which makes both die 'as soon as they seed', and the notion of angels lying lieger which he borrowed from Herbert. Apart from these the poem makes very little show of intellectual wit, and in the movement towards pastoral in the middle section—felt especially in the rhyme 'mountain . . . fountain' which proposes itself so obviously—Vaughan seems to be reverting to a much less demanding tradition. The metaphysical structure of *Corruption* is firm enough to carry such relaxed writing, but a final assessment of this poem will recognize how much it dilutes the style which for Donne is so potent and concentrated a medium of expression.

Andrew Marvell

To his Coy Mistress

Had we but world enough, and time,
This coyness, lady, were no crime.
We would sit down and think which way
To walk and pass our long love's day.
Thou by the Indian Ganges' side
Shouldst rubies find; I by the tide
Of Humber would complain. I would
Love you ten years before the Flood;
And you should, if you please, refuse
10 Till the conversion of the Jews.
My vegetable love should grow
Vaster than empires, and more slow.
An hundred years should go to praise
Thine eyes, and on thy forehead gaze;
Two hundred to adore each breast;
But thirty thousand to the rest:
An age at least to every part,
And the last age should show your heart.
For, lady, you deserve this state;
20 Nor would I love at lower rate.
    But at my back I always hear
Time's winged chariot hurrying near;
And yonder all before us lie
Deserts of vast eternity.
Thy beauty shall no more be found,
Nor, in thy marble vault, shall sound
My echoing song. Then worms shall try
That long-preserved virginity,
And your quaint honour turn to dust,
30 And into ashes all my lust.
The grave's a fine and private place,
But none, I think, do there embrace.
    Now, therefore, while the youthful hue
Sits on thy skin like morning dew,
And while thy willing soul transpires
At every pore with instant fires,
Now let us sport us while we may;
And now, like amorous birds of prey,
Rather at once our time devour
40 Than languish in his slow-chapt power.
Let us roll all our strength, and all
Our sweetness up into one ball,
And tear our pleasures with rough strife
Thorough the iron gates of life.
Thus, though we may not make our sun
Stand still, yet we will make him run.

Concentration is a prominent feature of Marvell's address *To his Coy Mistress*, but although his poem has been lavishly praised as 'the very roof and crown of the metaphysical love lyric', in other important respects it lies at a considerable distance from the line of Donne. The likenesses are clear enough. Like *The Flea*, it attempts to break the lady's resistance by means of a witty argument, whose stages are indicated by the initial phrases of its three sections: 'Had we . . . But . . . Now, therefore.' Each of these sections has a distinctive tone and mood—relaxed indulgence, terror, and fierce determination—and its own pace; and Marvell does not attempt to combine these strongly disparate elements into a continuous design. Each is completely at variance with the other two, and the dramatic shock of juxtaposition repeats an effect often encountered in Donne. The language is terse and compressed, and packed into the confined space of an octosyllabic line as though to give it still greater explosive force. A succession of witty images and figures gives the whole poem the sense of an exactly controlled and pointed statement, and suggests a speaker whose intellect is keenly alive to the absurdities of his passion as well as to the desperate need for haste. The same kind of wit prompts Donne to make fun of himself in *The Relic* despite the seriousness of his feelings for the woman. Again like *The Relic*, Marvell's poem involves an incongruous and macabre association of the lover's passion with the grave; though the grim particularity of Marvell's references to vaults and worms helps to make his poem much more disturbing than Donne's. The fear which these images evoke serves his purpose of driving the lady towards surrender; and the poem ends with the sense of dialectical triumph which, for Marvell as for Donne, represents the achievement of this purpose.

In these respects *To his Coy Mistress* deserves to be recognized as a metaphysical poem; but in other ways it must be seen as the product of a very different literary tradition. The central theme of the poem—sexual conquest of a reluctant mistress—owes much less to Donne than to Catullus, whose ideas are taken up more delicately by Jonson in the song,

> Come, my Celia, let us prove
> While we may the sports of love.

Here, as in Marvell's poem, the speaker warns the lady that they have little time to spare, and that once their sun has set "tis with us perpetual night'. Donne makes no use of this argument: he sets out to demonstrate to his mistress that her resistance is logically indefensible, and not to frighten her with reminders that her beauty must fade and that she may carry her virginity uselessly to the grave. Such appeals through emotion are alien to Donne, who intends to carry the fortress by sheer weight of intellectual proof. Marvell adopts the very different technique of arousing powerful instinctive feelings through the use of emotionally charged language, which is a common poetic practice and not characteristic of metaphysical writing. Thus when he suggest to the lady (lines 5–6):

> Thou by the Indian Ganges' side
> Should'st rubies find;

or promises that his 'vegetable love' will grow 'Vaster than empires, and more slow' (line 12) Marvell depends for his immediate effect not upon witty ideas but upon a succession of rich vowel-sounds, which build up an impression of luxury and abundance. In the next section of the poem, the image of 'Time's winged chariot hurrying near' (line 22) catches the sense of rapid movement through its beating rhythm and its blurring of syllables in 'chariot' and 'hurrying', which are both rendered as trochees.* That the poem contains several strikingly witty conceits will not be denied. There are flashes of wry humour which Donne might have inspired, like the mock-solemn proposal to adore each breast for two centuries, or the self-derisive description of the lover complaining 'by the tide of Humber'—a river-setting as prosaic as the Ganges is exotic. At least one passage recalls Donne in its savage outspokenness, and here the weight of meaning brought to bear on the verb—'Then worms shall try/That long-preserved virginity' (lines 27–8)—shows the intellectual sharpness which characterizes metaphysical poetry as Donne has written it. What most distinguishes the poem from the work of Marvell's great predecessor is the lack of originality in its central theme, or—to be more complimentary to Marvell—its indebtedness to a tradition of European poetry running back to Roman times. We are unlikely to have read anything remotely resembling *The Flea* or *The Relic*: poems which Dr Johnson might have had in mind when he remarked that the reader 'wonders more frequently by what perverseness of industry' the metaphysical poets managed to hit upon their strange ideas. On the other hand the theme of *Carpe diem* (snatch the day and hour) which Marvell exploits with such energy and novelty of manner in *To his Coy Mistress* was a commonplace of early seventeenth-century poetry, at which most of Jonson's disciples tried their hands. Where Donne is brilliantly individual, Marvell contrives a happy compromise between an unmistakably personal style and a theme which is part of the common heritage of European poets. The line of English lyric poetry is being led back from the extremism of Donne's writing, with its often clamorous insistence upon the uniqueness of speaker and event, towards a quieter mode of expression and the recognition of cultural links with the past which were to seem increasingly important as the seventeenth century progressed. In this movement not Donne but Jonson was the leader; and although Marvell's bizarre concepts and passionate energy show one influence, his appeal to the coy mistress admits a respectful familiarity with a perennial theme of poetry and a readiness to work within the tradition which Jonson had revived.

---

*That is, each loses one of its unstressed syllables, so that—∪∪ becomes—∪ charr-yot, hurr-ying. The line is really decasyllabic, with five stresses, and has been compressed into four metrical feet.

Short Biographies

BACON, FRANCIS, BARON VERULAM, 1561–1626. Educated at Cambridge and Gray's Inn. Between 1607 and 1618 he was appointed successively solicitor-general, attorney-general and lord chancellor. In 1621 he was found guilty of bribery and deprived of office. He published his *Essays* in 1597, with an augmented edition in 1625; but the writing for which he is chiefly remembered consists of scientific and philosophical works in English and Latin, notably *The Advancement of Learning* 1605 and the *Novum Organum* 1620. These gave considerable impetus to the interests which led to a new scientific outlook later in the century.

BEDFORD, LUCY COUNTESS OF. Date of birth uncertain: she married Edward Russell, third earl of Bedford, in 1594, and died in 1627. She was Donne's friend and patroness from 1608 until her death. Many of his letters and at least eight of his poems are addressed to her. *A Nocturnal upon St Lucy's Day* may allude to her, and she is more certainly the woman to whom *Twickenham Garden* refers. Ben Jonson and Drayton were among those who addressed complimentary poems to her.

BROOKE, CHRISTOPHER, *c.* 1575–1627. As a young man he studied at Lincoln's Inn, where he shared a chamber with Donne, who addressed *The Storm* to him. Together with his brother Samuel, who acted as priest at Donne's wedding, he was imprisoned for his part in the ceremony. He became a bencher of his Inn, but kept up his connection with the literary world: he published elegies, an eclogue and a work called *The Ghost of Richard III*.

BROWNE, SIR THOMAS, 1605–82. Practised as a physician at Norwich after studying at Oxford and several continental universities. His *Religio Medici* was written in 1635 and published in 1643: *Vulgar Errors* appeared in 1646 and *Urn Burial* in 1658. He was knighted during a royal visit to Norwich in 1671.

CAREW, THOMAS, *c.* 1598–1639. Educated at Oxford, was secretary to the ambassador at Venice and then appointed to an office at Court by Charles I. One of the 'tribe of Ben' who wrote a masque and many songs and lyrics, published in 1640. His name is pronounced 'carey'.

CLEVELAND, JOHN, 1613–58. A Leicestershire man educated at Cambridge, where he attracted the attention of Charles I by his speech during a royal visit. A vehement royalist, he was ejected from his college fellowship by parliamentary visitors and joined the king's forces at Oxford. His political satires made a great impression, in particular his scathing attack on the Scots. His non-satirical writing includes an elegy on Milton's friend Edward King.

DANVERS, SIR JOHN, *c.* 1588–1655. The second husband of Magdalen Herbert, whom he married in 1608 when she was more than twice his age. In 1625 he was elected M.P. for Oxford, and continued to sit in Parliament until the civil war. He sided with the parliamentary party, and became sufficiently prominent to be one of the signatories to Charles I's death-warrant.

DENHAM, SIR JOHN, 1615–69. Born in Dublin and educated at Oxford: a royalist who was compelled to surrender Farnham Castle to the parliamentary forces in 1642. In the same year he published *Cooper's Hill*, a topographical poem containing an address to the Thames whose terms were adopted as the critical standard of urbane writing later in the seventeenth century.

DRUMMOND OF HAWTHORNDEN, WILLIAM, 1585–1649. Born near Edinburgh, where he was educated. He was a friend of Drayton and an acquaintance of Ben Jonson, who visited him in 1619. He recorded Jonson's remarks about literature and contemporary poets; these *Conversations* hold more interest today than Drummond's original writing, which included poems and a history of Scotland.

DRURY, SIR ROBERT, 1577–1615. Educated at Cambridge for a time, then became a soldier and was knighted in the field at seventeen. He was again fighting in the Low Countries in 1597, and later served in Ireland. His hopes of a diplomatic career did not materialise, possibly because his hot temper stood against him. After the death of his daughter Elizabeth in December 1610 he became friend and patron to Donne, who accompanied him on a journey abroad in 1611–12.

EGERTON, SIR THOMAS, *c.* 1540–1617. After studying at Lincoln's Inn he rapidly acquired fame as a lawyer. In 1581 he was appointed solicitor-general, and in 1592 attorney-general. Francis Bacon, whom he was to succeed as lord chancellor, acknowledged his 'fatherly care' of young barristers. Egerton become lord keeper in 1596. A close friend of Essex, he was one of the officers of state locked up in Essex's house during the abortive uprising of 1601, and he took a prominent part in the trial which followed.

GOODYER, SIR HENRY, 1571–1628. One of Donne's closest friends, to whom he wrote very frequently. One of the *Letters to Several Personages* is addressed to him from Mitcham. Goodyer was elected M.P. for a Cornish constituency in 1603, and was knighted in the same year after being made one of the gentlemen of the king's privy chamber. He seems to have lived extravagantly after this, and to have run into difficulties which Donne eased by a gift of money.

HARVEY, WILLIAM, 1578–1657. Educated at Canterbury and Cambridge. He first revealed his discovery of the circulation of the blood in a lecture to the College of Physicians in 1616, but did not publish his treatise until 1628. As physician to Charles I, he was present with him at the battle of Edgehill in 1642.

HERBERT, GEORGE, 1593–1633. After his education at Westminster and Cambridge he followed the court, and was appointed public orator of his university. A few years before his death he withdrew from courtly life and entered the priesthood, living very simply as rector of Bemerton in Wiltshire, where he died. His religious poems were published in 1633 as *The Temple*. His elder brother Edward (HERBERT OF CHERBURY 1583–1648), distinguished himself as philosopher, historian, poet and diplomat. Their mother, Magdalen Herbert, was widowed in 1597 and in 1608 married Sir John Danvers. Donne's correspondence with her, and presumably his first acquaintance, dates from 1607. She died in 1627.

HEYWOOD, JOHN, C. 1497–1580. Donne's grandfather on his mother's side. At first a chorister and court musician, he was later a writer of interludes and entertainments, which included the comedy *The Four Ps*. He was a favourite of Mary I, who enjoyed his wit. At the accession of the protestant Elizabeth he went into exile. At least five editions of his *Epigrams* were published in the early years of her reign.

JONES, INIGO, 1573–1652. Architect who introduced classical style into England. He was responsible for several important London buildings, notably the Banqueting House in Whitehall and the Queen's House at Greenwich. He also designed costumes, decor and machines for court masques by Jonson, Heywood, D'Avenant and others.

JONSON, BEN, 1572–1637. Educated at Westminster, then followed his stepfather's trade as bricklayer and saw military service in Flanders. In 1597 he joined Shakespeare's company as an actor. His *Everyman in his Humour* was performed a year later. The first of his many masques was presented at court in 1605, with scenery by Inigo Jones. James I granted him a pension in 1616 after his major comedies *The Alchemist, Volpone* and *Bartholomew Fair* had been written and staged. A friend of Shakespeare, Bacon, Donne, Chapman and many other writers. His critical opinions, published in 1641 as *Discoveries*, were taken up by the 'tribe' of young poets now called Cavaliers, and influenced the development of a lucid and impersonal poetic style.

KER, SIR ROBERT, 1578–1654. A courtier who accompanied James I to England in 1603. He was made personal attendant to Prince Henry, and under Charles I master of the privy purse. In 1639 he was awarded a pension of £2000 and given the title of Earl of Ancrum; but the civil war reduced him to poverty and he fled to Holland, where he died in debt. Donne gave him a copy of his *Biathanatos* and an MS collection of his poems before going to Germany in 1619, and wrote many letters to him.

KING, HENRY, 1592–1669. Educated at Westminster and Oxford. He took orders, and after being a prebendary of St. Paul's during Donne's years as dean, became bishop of Chichester. A personal friend of

Donne, whose will he executed, and of Jonson and Walton. He wrote and published poems, of which the verses addressed to his dead wife are the most famous.

LOVELACE, RICHARD, 1618–58. Educated at Charterhouse and Oxford: a wealthy and handsome courtier who fought for the king after being imprisoned by parliament in 1642, when he presented the so-called Kentish petition. He was imprisoned again in 1648, and spent the time preparing his *Lucasta*—a collection of lyrics, songs and odes—for publication in 1649. He seems to have died in want.

LYLY, JOHN, *c.* 1554–1606. One of the 'university wits' of the English renaissance. After studying at Oxford he published the first part of *Euphues* in 1578, a prose tale whose preposterously mannered style impelled the literary fashion of 'euphuism'. Subsequently he wrote a series of urbanely witty comedies which were privately staged by boy actors; notably *Compasbe, Endymion* and *Mother Bombie*.

MARVELL, ANDREW, 1621–78. Educated at Hull and Cambridge. After spending four years on the continent, partly at Rome, in 1651 he became tutor to the daughter of Lord Fairfax, at whose country house near York he probably wrote his poems praising country life and retirement. These were not published until 1681. After the Restoration he was M.P. for Hull and a political satirist.

MORE, GEORGE, 1553–1632. Father of Ann More, Donne's wife. After studying at Oxford and the Inner Temple, he was elected M.P. for Guildford and knighted in 1597. A year later he became sheriff of Surrey and Sussex. James I appointed him a chamberlain and treasurer to Prince Henry; and in 1615 he became lieutenant of the Tower of London.

MORTON, THOMAS, 1564–1659. Educated at York, where he was at school with Guy Fawkes, and Cambridge. He took orders in 1592, and proceeded D.D. in 1606. From being a university lecturer in logic, he rose to be a chaplain to James I, dean of Winchester, and bishop successively of Chester, Litchfield and Durham. He published over twenty works, some in Latin, showing the fallaciousness of Catholic doctrine, always in temperate terms.

SIDNEY family. Chiefly remembered for Sir Philip Sidney, 1554–86, courtier, soldier and poet, whose *Arcadia, Apology for Poetry* and *Astrophel and Stella* characterize the spirit of the English renaissance. The family estate at Penshurst, which passed into other hands at the marriage of Sir Philip's niece, was the subject of two complimentary poems by Jonson.

VAUGHAN, HENRY, 1622–95. Educated at Oxford and London, where he studied law. After the civil war, in which he fought as a royalist, he practised as a physician at Brecknock. His best work as a poet was published in 1650 and 1655 as *Silex Scintillans* (sparkling flint); contemplative and half-mystical pieces rather than directly religious in the manner of Donne and Herbert.

WALTON, IZAAK, 1593–1683. London ironmonger, the friend of Donne, Henry King and Sir Henry Wotton. He is chiefly remembered for his *Compleat Angler*, 1653, and for the biographies of Donne, Herbert, Hooker and Wotton which were published together in 1670.

WEBSTER, JOHN, *c.* 1580–1625. The son of a London tailor who turned to the stage, and became one of the outstanding Jacobean dramatists. His first plays were comedies, but in *The White Devil* and *The Duchess of Malfi* he proved his power as a writer of sombre tragedy which mirrored the pessimism of his age.

Select bibliography

Biography

IZAAK, WALTON, *Life of Donne*, 1640. Available in World's Classics, Oxford U.P., 1927.

R. C. BALD, *John Donne: A Life*, Oxford U.P. 1970.

Editions of Donne's work

Poems, ed. H. J. C. Grierson, Oxford U.P., 1912, one volume ed. 1929.

Elegies and Songs and Sonets, ed. Helen Gardner, Oxford U.P. 1965.

Songs and Sonets, ed. Theodore Redpath, Methuen, 1956.

Donne, ed. John Hayward, Penguin Poets, 1956.

The Divine Poems, ed. Helen Gardner, Oxford U.P., 1953.

Satires, Epigrams and Verse Letters, ed. W. Milgate, Oxford U.P. 1967.

Complete Poetry and Selected Prose, ed. John Hayward, 4th edn, Faber, (Nonesuch library) 1955.

Critical studies

ALVAREZ, A. *The School of Donne*, Chatto and Windus, 1961.

BENNETT, JOAN, *Five Metaphysical Poets*, Cambridge U.P. 1964.

GRANSDEN, K. W., *John Donne*, Longmans (Men and Books), 1954.

MARTZ, L. *Poetry of Meditation*, Yale U.P. 1954, rev. 1962.

LEISHMAN, J. B., *Donne: the Monarch of Wit*, Hutchinson University Library 5th ed. 1962.

RUGOFF, M. A., *Donne's Imagery*, New York, privately printed, 1939.

SIMPSON, E. M., *A Study of the Prose Works of Donne*, Oxford U.P. 1924, rev. 1948.

SPENCER, T., and others, *A Garland for John Donne*, New York 1932.

STEIN, A. *John Donne's Lyrics*, Minnesota U.P. 1962.

TUVE, ROSAMUND, *Elisabethan and Metaphysical Imagery*, Chicago U.P. 1947. Phoenix ed. 1961.

UNGER, L. *Donne's Poetry and Modern Criticism*, Chicago U.P. 1962.

Anthologies

Metaphysical Lyrics and Poems, ed. H. J. C. Grierson, Oxford U.P., 1921.

The Metaphysical Poets, ed. Helen Gardner, Penguin Poets, 1957.

Dr. Johnson's essay on metaphysical poetry appears under 'Abraham Cowley' in *Lives of the English Poets* 1779–81, reprinted in Everyman's Library. The essay by T. S. Eliot is included in the *Collected Essays*, Faber and Faber, 1931.

Index